BASIC / NOT BORING MATH SKILLS

FRACTIONS & DECIMALS

Grades 6–8+

Inventive Exercises to Sharpen
Skills and Raise Achievement

Series Concept & Development
by Imogene Forte & Marjorie Frank
Exercises by Terri Breeden & Andrea Sukow

Incentive Publications, Inc.
Nashville, Tennessee

About the cover:
Bound resist, or tie dye, is the most ancient known method of fabric surface design. The brilliance of the basic tie dye design on this cover reflects the possibilities that emerge from the mastery of basic skills.

Illustrated by Kathleen Bullock
Cover art by Mary Patricia Deprez, dba Tye Dye Mary®
Cover design by Marta Drayton, Joe Shibley, and W. Paul Nance
Edited by Anna Quinn

ISBN 0-86530-370-3

PRINTED IN THE UNITED STATES OF AMERICA

TABLE OF CONTENTS

INTRODUCTION . . . Celebrate Basic Math Skills 7

    Skills Checklist for Fractions & Decimals 8

SKILLS EXERCISES 9

    It's a Dog's Life . . . (Identify Fractional Parts) 10

    Which Winter Wear? . . . (Fractional & Mixed Numbers) 11

    High-Speed Sporting . . . (Compare & Order Fractions) 12

    Homework First . . . (Convert Mixed Numerals & Fractions) 13

    Red & White or Black & Blue . . . (Identify Factors and Multiples) ... 14

    Foul Weather or Fowl Weather? . . . (Greatest Common Factors) 15

    At the Top . . . (Identify Multiples) 16

    Famous Words . . . (Identify Equivalent Fractions) 17

    Top 10 Questions . . . (Identify Equivalent Fractions) 18

    Weighing In . . . (Fractions in Lowest Terms) 19

    Friday Night Football . . . (Add & Subtract Fractions) 20

    Fractions in a Backpack . . . (Add & Subtract Fractions) 22

    Dangerous Fractions . . . (Add & Subtract Mixed Numerals) 23

    Great-Tasting Awards . . . (Multiply Fractions) 24

    That Fish Was HOW Big? . . . (Multiply Mixed Numerals) 25

    What's Cookin' on the Campfire? . . . (Multiply Mixed Numerals) ... 26

    Crashing Not Intended . . . (Divide Fractions) 27

    Read It Right! . . . (Read & Write Decimals) 28

High-Speed Records . . . (Compare & Order Decimals) 30

Amazing Speed Facts . . . (Identify Place Value in Decimals) 31

Well-Rounded Athletes . . . (Round Decimals) 32

Take to the Slopes . . . (Add & Subtract Decimals) 33

Springboard to Decimals . . . (Multiply & Add Decimals) 34

Three Times the Work . . . (Divide Decimals) 35

Face Off! . . . (Change Fractions to Decimals) 36

A Boxing Legend Speaks . . . (Change Decimals to Fractions) 37

Birds That Count . . . (Convert Decimals & Percents) 38

Musical Statistics . . . (Convert Fractions & Percents) 39

Off the Tee . . . (Convert Fractions & Percents) 40

Can You Canoe? . . . (Solve Problems with Percents) 41

Lost: Softball Stats . . . (Solve Problems with Percents) 42

On to Wimbledon? . . . (Write Ratios) 43

And They're Off! . . . (Determine Rate & Write Ratios) 44

Are We Lost—Or What? . . . (Solve Proportions) 45

Underground Explorations . . . (Read & Write Proportions) 46

Highs & Lows . . . (Solve Problems with Fractions & Decimals) 48

A Matter of Seconds . . . (Solve Problems with Decimals) 49

More Top 10 Questions . . . (Solve Problems with Fractions & Decimals) 50

APPENDIX 51

Glossary 53

Fractions & Decimals Skills Test 56

Skills Test Answer Key 59

Answers 60

CELEBRATE BASIC MATH SKILLS

Basic does not mean boring! There certainly is nothing dull about using fascinating sports situations or fractions and decimals to . . .

> . . . get to know who's who in the TOP 10 lists of medal-winning athletes
>
> . . . find out which bobsleds in the Olympics are longest, lightest, and fastest
>
> . . . unravel mystery quotes by great athletes
>
> . . . calculate greatest sports accomplishments, injuries, disasters, and winners
>
> . . . help athletes and adventurers pack their backpacks, reduce their weight, or paddle a canoe
>
> . . . avoid disaster on a mountain-climbing or cave-exploring expedition
>
> . . . figure out how much hikers will eat around the campfire
>
> . . . predict which cars will crash at a stock car race
>
> . . . track speeds of swimmers, runners, skiers, and even elevators
>
> . . . solve problems with sled dogs, race horses, scuba divers, and athletes' salaries

The idea of celebrating the basics is just what it sounds like—enjoying and improving the basic skills for solving math problems. The pages that follow are full of exercises for students that will help to review and strengthen specific, basic skills in the content area of math. This is not just another ordinary "fill-in-the-blanks" way to learn. The high-interest activities will put students to work applying a rich variety of skills related to fractions and decimals as they enjoy fun, challenging adventures with numbers, ideas, and sports-related dilemmas.

The pages in this book can be used in many ways:
- by individual students to sharpen a particular skill
- with a small group needing to relearn or strengthen a skill
- as an instructional tool for teaching a skill to any size group
- by students working on their own
- by students working under the direction of an adult

Each page may be used to introduce a new skill, reinforce a skill, or assess a student's performance of a skill. As students take on the challenges of these adventures with problems, they will grow in their mastery of basic skills and will enjoy learning to the fullest. And as you watch them check off the basic fraction and decimal skills they've strengthened, you can celebrate with them!

SKILLS CHECKLIST FOR FRACTIONS & DECIMALS

✔	SKILL	PAGE(S)
	Name fractional parts of a whole or set	10
	Read and write fractional numbers and mixed numerals	10, 11
	Compare and order fractions	12
	Write mixed numerals as fractions	13
	Identify factors, prime factors, and composite factors and multiples	14, 15, 16
	Identify common factors and greatest common factors	15
	Identify multiples and least common multiples	16
	Identify equivalent fractions	17, 18
	Identify and write fractions in lowest terms	19
	Add and subtract fractions with like denominators	20, 21, 22
	Add and subtract fractions with unlike denominators	20, 21, 22
	Add and subtract mixed numerals	23
	Multiply fractions	24
	Multiply mixed numerals	25, 26
	Divide fractions	27
	Read and write decimals and mixed numerals	28, 29, 30
	Compare and order decimals and mixed numerals	30
	Identify place value in decimals	31
	Round decimals	32
	Add and subtract decimals	33
	Multiply decimals	34
	Divide decimals	35, 48
	Change fractions to decimals	36
	Change decimals to fractions	37
	Understand, read, and write percents	38
	Write decimals as percents and percents as decimals	38, 39, 48, 50
	Write fractions as percents	40
	Solve problems to find percents	41, 42, 50
	Find the original number when the percent is known	42
	Compare numbers or quantities by writing ratios	43, 44, 50
	Define and determine rate and write rates as ratios	44
	Understand and write proportions	45, 46, 47
	Use cross multiplication to solve proportions	45, 46, 47
	Solve problems with decimals and fractions	48, 49, 50

FRACTIONS & DECIMALS

Skills Exercises

IT'S A DOG'S LIFE

The International Sled Dog Racing Association calls dogsledding the "world's fastest growing winter sport." Dog teams generally consist of 14 dogs, but can include as many as 20 dogs. Not every dog on the team is a husky. Many other breeds are used. Labradors, hounds, Irish setters, Alaskan malamutes, and non-purebred mixes are popular choices. Examine the dog teams below and answer the following questions.

Dog Team 1	Dog Team 2	Dog Team 3	Dog Team 4	Dog Team 5
4 Labradors	1 Labrador	8 Labradors	2 Labradors	1 Labrador
4 Alaskan malamutes	3 Alaskan malamutes	4 Alaskan malamutes	10 Alaskan malamutes	4 Alaskan malamutes
1 hound	1 hound	1 hound	2 huskies	2 huskies
1 Irish setter	2 Irish setters	1 Irish setter		5 non-purebred mixes
2 huskies	3 huskies			
2 non-purebred mixes	4 non-purebred mixes			

1. Team 1 has 14 dogs. Write a fraction that represents the ratio of the number of Labradors to the number of dogs on the whole team. _____

2. Team 1 has 14 dogs. Write a fraction that represents the number of Alaskan malamutes and huskies compared to the number of dogs on the whole team. _____

3. Team 2 has 14 dogs. Write a fraction that compares the number of Irish setters and huskies to the number of dogs on the whole team. _____

4. Team 2 has 14 dogs. Write a fraction that compares the number of huskies to the number of dogs on the whole team. _____

5. Team 3 has 14 dogs. Write a fraction that compares the number of Labradors and Alaskan malamutes to the number of dogs on the whole team. _____

6. In Teams 4 and 5 there are 26 dogs. Write a fraction that compares the number of Alaskan malamutes in both teams to the total number of dogs in both teams. _____

7. The number of dogs on all teams combined is 68. Complete the chart below to show how many of each breed are on the teams. Write a fraction for each breed.

Type of dog	Labrador	Alaskan malamute	Hound	Irish setter	Husky	Non-purebred
Fraction $\left(\dfrac{\text{Number in That Breed}}{\text{Total Number of Dogs}}\right)$						

Name _____

WHICH WINTER WEAR?

Maria is making choices about clothing for winter skiing and mountain-climbing adventures. She's comparing winter gear in several catalogs. Read and answer the questions below about the clothing she is considering buying.

_____ 1. In a clothing catalog the new Mountain Parkas boast that they are 65% polyester. Write this percent as a fraction.

_____ 2. The 3-layer parka is advertised as the warmest. All three layers are of equal weight. One of the layers is 100% wool. No other layers contain wool. What fraction shows how much of the jacket is wool?

_____ 3. When Maria called the catalog center she was told that over 365 of the parkas were sold. If they originally had 500 parkas, what fraction would show how many were sold?

_____ 4. The Gore-Tex Squall that sells for $295 is compared to other squalls that cost $500. Write a fraction that compares the inexpensive squall to the expensive squall.

_____ 5. One woman's parka is two and three-fourths times the cost of a similar one in another catalog. Write the mixed numeral represented by these words.

_____ 6. The ski club asked Maria to order pullovers for everyone. There are 10 members of the club, and 7 of them wanted green pullovers. Write a fraction to represent the number that wanted green pullovers.

_____ 7. The quilted, goose down vest is advertised to be 98% waterproof. What fraction does this percent represent?

_____ 8. Leather gloves come in the following sizes: eight and one-half, nine and one-half, and ten and one-half. Write these three sizes as mixed numerals.

_____ 9. The ear bands come in the following colors: navy, evergreen, garnet, and black. The catalog company stocked 200 of each color. If 77 are left, what fraction of the ear bands have been sold?

_____ 10. In the 233-page catalog, 10 pages are devoted to outerwear. Write a fraction that compares the number of outerwear pages to the entire catalog.

_____ 11. The ski pants Maria wants are $89 in the Outdoor Outlet Catalog. The same pants are $108 in another catalog. Write a fraction that shows the comparison of the more expensive to the less expensive pants.

_____ 12. The Winter Wear catalog does one-third the business that the Outdoor Adventurer does. Write a fraction showing the comparison of the Outdoor Adventurer to Winter Wear.

Name _____

HIGH-SPEED SPORTING

Bobsledding is a fast and dangerous winter sport. It's also one of the most thrilling. The sleds are made of aluminum and steel, and they travel up to 90 miles per hour. The length of each sled cannot exceed $12\frac{1}{2}$ feet.

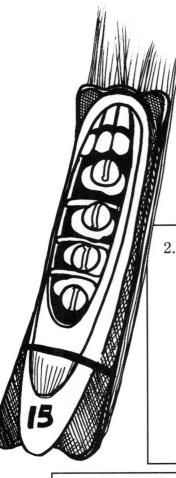

1. Place the sleds in order by their length. List these sleds from longest to shortest.

United States' sled	$11\frac{7}{8}$ feet	_____
Jamaica's sled	$12\frac{1}{3}$ feet	_____
Switzerland's sled	$11\frac{8}{9}$ feet	_____
Canada's sled	$12\frac{1}{2}$ feet	_____
Russia's sled	$11\frac{1}{4}$ feet	_____

2. The total weight allowed on a bobsled (including the crew) is 1,389 pounds. Place these sleds in order by their weight, listing them from the lightest to the heaviest.

United States	$1,333\frac{1}{2}$ lbs.	_____
Jamaica	$1,386\frac{1}{3}$ lbs.	_____
Switzerland	$1,386\frac{3}{4}$ lbs.	_____
Canada	$1,386\frac{1}{8}$ lbs.	_____
Russia	$1,333\frac{3}{4}$ lbs.	_____

3. Championship bobsled races consist of four heats. The team with the lowest composite (total) score wins. Total the following heats and circle the winning team.

United States	$2\frac{1}{2}$ minutes, 3 minutes, $3\frac{1}{2}$ minutes, and $2\frac{1}{2}$ minutes
Jamaica	$2\frac{1}{2}$ minutes, $2\frac{1}{2}$ minutes, $3\frac{1}{2}$ minutes, and $2\frac{1}{2}$ minutes
Switzerland	$2\frac{1}{3}$ minutes, 2 minutes, $2\frac{1}{2}$ minutes, and 3 minutes
Canada	2 minutes, $2\frac{1}{2}$ minutes, 2 minutes, and $2\frac{1}{3}$ minutes
Russia	$2\frac{3}{4}$ minutes, $2\frac{1}{2}$ minutes, $2\frac{1}{2}$ minutes, and 3 minutes

Name _____

HOMEWORK FIRST

You've got your roller blades over your shoulder and are ready to go out the door, when your mom yells, "You have to do your homework first." Quickly finish these fraction problems about skating time.

I. Each improper fraction gives a time that one skater spent on roller blades for the past 10 days. Rewrite each improper fraction as a whole number or a mixed numeral in simplest form.

1. $\frac{5}{2}$ hrs. _____

2. $\frac{8}{3}$ hrs. _____

3. $\frac{13}{4}$ hrs. _____

4. $\frac{11}{8}$ hrs. _____

5. $\frac{9}{3}$ hrs. _____

6. $\frac{12}{5}$ hrs. _____

7. $\frac{24}{7}$ hrs. _____

8. $\frac{3}{2}$ hrs. _____

9. $\frac{15}{2}$ hrs. _____

10. $\frac{13}{5}$ hrs. _____

II. Each mixed numeral gives an amount of time that you've spent skating in the last 10 days. Rewrite each mixed numeral as an improper fraction.

11. 1 and $\frac{1}{4}$ hrs. _____

12. 1 and $\frac{3}{4}$ hrs. _____

13. 2 and $\frac{1}{4}$ hrs. _____

14. 2 and $\frac{1}{5}$ hrs. _____

15. 2 and $\frac{4}{5}$ hrs. _____

16. 4 and $\frac{1}{5}$ hrs. _____

17. 1 and $\frac{1}{10}$ hrs. _____

18. 1 and $\frac{5}{10}$ hrs. _____

19. 3 and $\frac{1}{10}$ hrs. _____

20. 2 and $\frac{7}{8}$ hrs. _____

Name _____

RED & WHITE OR BLACK & BLUE

Basketball players may get black and blue if they have mishaps or make mistakes on the court. But if they make mistakes in math class, their papers will look pretty red and white. Take a look at the math paper of star basketball player Shaundra. She's trying to sort out factors, prime factors, and composite factors.

I. First, practice these concepts yourself. If you see a prime number, circle it in red. If you see a composite number, circle it in blue.

1. $12 = 2 \times 6$
2. $24 = 2 \times 2 \times 6$
3. $13 = 1 \times 13$
4. $36 = 2 \times 2 \times 3 \times 3$
5. $21 = 3 \times 7$
6. $28 = 2 \times 2 \times 7$
7. $56 = 7 \times 8$
8. $63 = 3 \times 3 \times 7$
9. $48 = 2 \times 2 \times 12$

II. Now look at Shaundra's paper. Her assignment was to factor all these numbers down to prime factors. Circle in blue all the ones she did correctly. In red, correct all her mistakes.

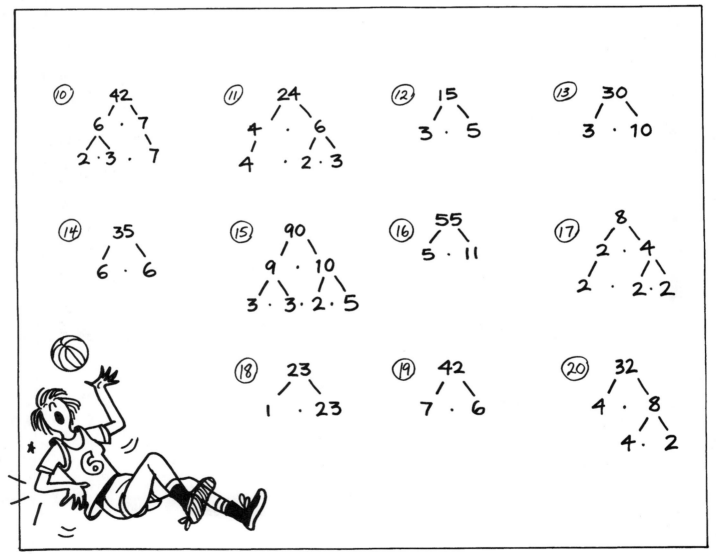

FOUL WEATHER OR FOWL WEATHER?

Whether you are an athlete engaged in an outdoor winter sport or just someone who spends a lot of time outside in the cold weather, you ought to know all about "cutis anserine." To determine what "cutis anserine" are, match the two numbers in the left column to their greatest common factor in the right column. (Remember: A common factor is a factor that two numbers share. A greatest common factor is the largest factor two numbers share!)

_____   1. GCF of 12 and 24   O.   8
_____   2 GCF of 8 and 36   E.   4
_____   3. GCF of 8 and 16   G. 12
_____   4. GCF of 13 and 39   P.   2
_____   5. GCF of 4 and 16   O.   8
_____   6. GCF of 10 and 25   B.   3
_____   7. GCF of 21 and 36   S. 13
_____   8. GCF of 5 and 15   U.   5
_____   9. GCF of 11 and 33   S. 13
_____ 10. GCF of 8 and 30   #.   5
_____ 11. GCF of 39 and 52   M. 11

So what are "cutis anserine"? _____

Solve these problems in a SNAP! (A cold snap, that is!)

_____ 12. GCF of 6 and 21
_____ 13. GCF of 12 and 15
_____ 14. GCF of 12 and 20
_____ 15. GCF of 7 and 35
_____ 16. GCF of 16 and 24
_____ 17. GCF of 9 and 15
_____ 18. GCF of 9 and 18
_____ 19. GCF of 18 and 20
_____ 20. GCF of 5 and 50

Name _____

AT THE TOP

To be at the top of their sports, these champions have won multiple titles or records. Use the numbers on these top 10 lists to practice identifying multiples.

WOMEN'S TOP 10 GRAND SLAM SINGLES WINNERS

	# of titles
Margaret Court	24
Helen Wills-Moody	19
Chris Evert-Lloyd	18
Martina Navratilova	18
Steffi Graf	18
Billie Jean King	12
Maureen Connolly	9
Suzanne Lenglen	8
Molla Mallory	8
Monica Seles	8

TOP 10 WORLD GOLF WINNERS OF MAJORS

	# of wins
Jack Nicklaus	18
Walter Hagen	11
Ben Hogan	9
Gary Player	9
Tom Watson	8
Harry Varden	7
Gene Sarazen	7
Bobby Jones	7
Sam Snead	7
Arnold Palmer	7

TOP 10 WINNING GRAND PRIX DRIVERS

	# of wins
Alain Prost	51
Ayrton Senna	41
Nigel Mansell	31
Jackie Stewart	27
Jim Clark	25
Niki Lauda	25
Juan Fangio	24
Nelson Piquet	23
Michael Schumacher	18
Stirling Moss	16

TOP 10 MALE (singles) FIGURE SKATERS
(World & Olympic Titles)

Ulrich Salchow	11
Karl Schafer	9
Dick Button	7
Gillis Grafstrom	6
Hayes Jenkins	5
Scott Hamilton	5
Willy Bockl	4
David Jenkins	4
Ondrej Nepela	4
Kurt Browning	4

1. List the 3 lowest common multiples of the totals of the 10th athletes in tennis and skating.____

2. What is the least common multiple of the top 3 figure skaters' number of titles? _____

3. List the 2 lowest common multiples of Steffi Graf, Gary Player, and Karl Schafer. _____

4. Margaret Court's total is a common multiple of which other players' totals?

_____

5. What is the least common multiple of Scott Hamilton's, Jim Clark's, and Monica Seles' totals?

_____

6. Chris Evert-Lloyd's total is the least common multiple of which players' totals?

_____

Name _____

FAMOUS WORDS

Lawrence Peter "Yogi" Berra won the American Baseball League's Most Valuable Player Award three times—1951, 1954, and 1955. Most folks also remember him for his famous, unpredictable comments. To discover one of his most famous sayings, match each fraction above to an equivalent fraction below.

(Don't worry if you see an alphabet letter several times. That just means that the letter is used several different times in Mr. Berra's famous comment and that the fractions are equivalent, too.) Dots represent spaces between words.

$$\frac{1}{2} \quad \frac{1}{3} \quad \frac{1}{4} \quad \frac{1}{5} \quad \frac{1}{2} \quad \frac{1}{6} \quad \frac{1}{9} \quad \frac{1}{3} \quad \frac{1}{4} \quad \frac{1}{7} \quad \frac{2}{5} \quad \frac{3}{5} \quad \frac{5}{6} \quad \frac{1}{4}$$

$$\frac{1}{9} \quad \frac{1}{3} \quad \frac{1}{2} \quad \frac{4}{5} \quad \frac{1}{4} \quad \frac{1}{2} \quad \frac{1}{3} \quad \frac{1}{9} \quad \frac{2}{3} \quad \frac{1}{4} \quad \frac{1}{7} \quad \frac{2}{5} \quad \frac{3}{5} \quad \frac{5}{6} \cdot$$

N = $^2/_{12}$	A = $^2/_{10}$	T = $^4/_{12}$	O = $^2/_{14}$	I = $^5/_{10}$	$'$ = $^3/_{27}$	V = $^6/_{15}$
T = $^8/_{24}$	I = $^4/_8$	$\cdot$ = $^2/_8$	V = $^{10}/_{25}$	L = $^8/_{10}$	R = $^{10}/_{12}$	E = $^9/_{15}$
T = $^2/_6$	$\cdot$ = $^4/_{16}$	S = $^4/_6$	R = $^{15}/_{18}$	$\cdot$ = $^{10}/_{40}$	$\cdot$ = $^{12}/_{48}$	E = $^6/_{10}$
I = $^3/_6$	$'$ = $^2/_{18}$	$\cdot$ = $^6/_{24}$	T = $^6/_{18}$	I = $^6/_{12}$	O = $^3/_{21}$	$'$ = $^4/_{36}$

Little League Baseball ..."it's wonderful, it keeps the kids out of the house."

A famous restaurant ....."Nobody goes there anymore. It's too crowded."

A famous Opera House ...."It was pretty good. Even the music was nice."

TOP 10 QUESTIONS

Here are 10 top questions about some top 10 topics in sports. You'll need to be in top shape with your understanding of equivalent fractions to answer these correctly. Choose your answers from the fractions sprinkled around the page.

$\frac{1}{5}$

$\frac{12}{52}$

$\frac{45}{50}$

$\frac{14}{20}$

$\frac{9}{21}$

$\frac{6}{20}$

$\frac{3}{5}$

$\frac{25}{110}$

$\frac{5}{18}$

$\frac{19}{11}$

$\frac{15}{30}$

$\frac{19}{10}$

$\frac{3}{5}$

$\frac{11}{44}$

1. Of the 10 most common sports injuries, 6 are specific to legs and knees. What fraction is equivalent to this ratio of $^6/_{10}$? _____

2. 5 of the 10 highest-earning sports movies feature boxing. Which fraction is equivalent to this ratio?_____

3. Over 40 million households watched Super Bowl XVI, the biggest TV audience ever for a sports event through 1996. Of the top 10 most-watched sporting events, 8 others were Super Bowls. What fraction shows the ratio of Super Bowls to the total of 10?_____

4. Riots, stampedes, crushes, collapsed stands, and fires at soccer games make up 7 of the top 10 worst disasters at sports events in the 20th century. What fraction shows the ratio of non-soccer disasters to soccer disasters? _____

5. In the 10 worst disasters at sports events, about 1900 people were killed. Approximately 1000 of these deaths happened at soccer events. What fraction shows this ratio? _____

6. The top 10 Olympic medal–winning countries in bobsledding have won a total of 90 medals. Switzerland holds 25 of these. What fraction shows the ratio of Switzerland's medals to the total?_____

7. U.S. Figure skater Kristi Yamaguchi, one of the top 10 world and Olympic title holders for women, holds 3 titles. Katarina Witt holds 6. Sonja Heine is number one with 13.
   a. What fraction shows the ratio of Kristi's to Katarina's titles? _____
   b. What fraction shows the ratio of Kristi's to Sonja's? _____

8. In the list of top 10 winners of the World Series, the NY Yankees are first with 22 wins. The Boston Red Sox are #5 with 5 wins. What fraction shows the ratio of Boston to NY? _____

9. In the list of the top 10 Olympic medal–winning countries, the U.S. at # 1 has over 1900. The USSR/CIS has over 1100. What fraction shows the U.S. to USSR/CIS ratio? _____

10. Of the top 10 highest-paid sportsmen in the world in 1995, 2 were basketball players. What fraction shows the ratio of basketball players to non-basketball sportsmen?_____

Name _____

WEIGHING IN!

Many athletes have to pay attention to their weight to participate in athletics. Some athletes, such as football players, wrestlers, or fighters, may wish to increase weight. In many cases, athletes are trying to reduce their weight. These fractions are a bit "weighty." They need reducing. In each case, reduce them to their lowest terms.

1. $4/8$ _____

2. $12/16$ _____

3. $20/25$ _____

4. $15/30$ _____

5. $2/6$ _____

6. $3/9$ _____

7. $9/27$ _____

8. $12/15$ _____

9. $36/42$ _____

10. $2/4$ _____

11. $2/8$ _____

12. $6/8$ _____

13. $4/8$ _____

14. $2/12$ _____

15. $8/20$ _____

16. $10/25$ _____

17. $25/35$ _____

18. $32/36$ _____

19. $20/55$ _____

20. $12/21$ _____

21. $15/18$ _____

22. $6/9$ _____

23. $3/12$ _____

24. $25/30$ _____

25. $30/48$ _____

26. $50/100$ _____

27. $9/24$ _____

28. $13/39$ _____

29. $8/16$ _____

30. $4/18$ _____

Reduced or **Not Reduced**? That is the question.

Circle all the fractions that are reduced to lowest terms. If a fraction is not reduced to lowest terms, reduce it and write your answer beside the fraction.

31. $\dfrac{13}{26}$ 32. $\dfrac{14}{42}$ 33. $\dfrac{8}{56}$ 34. $\dfrac{21}{63}$ 35. $\dfrac{5}{23}$ 36. $\dfrac{4}{21}$ 37. $\dfrac{30}{45}$ 38. $\dfrac{6}{23}$

Name _____

Basic Skills/Fractions & Decimals 6-8+

FRIDAY NIGHT FOOTBALL

East Middle School's football team is getting beaten badly by Franklin Middle School. The score is 42 to 10. Sherry and Elizabeth are bored with the game, but they have to stay until their older brother comes to pick them up. Maybe the time will go faster if they try to figure out the answers to these dilemmas. (Use the sketch of a football field on page 21 to help you solve problems.) Give your answers in fractions, whole numbers, or mixed numerals.

_____ 1. The first field goal East Middle School makes is $2\frac{1}{4}$ minutes into the first quarter. If the clock starts counting down at 12 minutes, how much time is left on the clock when this field goal is scored?

_____ 2. The second quarter starts and the clock is reset to 12 minutes. Franklin's first touchdown is made $3\frac{1}{4}$ minutes into the quarter. Another touchdown is made $5\frac{3}{4}$ minutes later. How much time is left in the second quarter when the second touch down is scored?

_____ 3. East scores their final touchdown $1\frac{1}{2}$ minutes into the third quarter. If the clock is reset to 12 at the beginning of each quarter, how many minutes are left after the East touchdown?

_____ 4. Franklin Middle School gains the following yards during one of their periods of possession: $12\frac{1}{2}$ yards, $9\frac{1}{2}$ yards, $32\frac{1}{2}$ yards, 2 yards, and $25\frac{1}{2}$ yards. How many yards are gained by Franklin Middle School?

_____ 5. East Middle School has possession of the ball on the 50-yard line. The team gains $11\frac{1}{4}$ yards. In the next play the ball is intercepted by Franklin's team and they run the ball $33\frac{3}{4}$ yards towards their goal. Where is the ball placed for the next play? Is it closer to Franklin's or East's goal? (Use the football field sketch to help with this problem.)

6. The sportswriter for the East School newspaper is writing an article for the paper. He is highlighting the players listed below. To help the sportswriter, use the information in the chart below and total the players' yards gained.

Yards Gained

Lightning Larry	$12\frac{3}{4}$ yds.	$7\frac{1}{4}$ yds.	2 yds.	_____ total
Cool-Kick Kerry	7 yds.	$2\frac{1}{2}$ yds.	$4\frac{1}{2}$ yds.	_____ total
Jumpin' Joe	$33\frac{1}{4}$ yds.	$2\frac{3}{4}$ yds.	10 yds.	_____ total
Speedy Sam	23 yds.	$3\frac{1}{3}$ yds.	$4\frac{2}{3}$ yds.	_____ total

Use with page 21.

Name

Use with page 20.

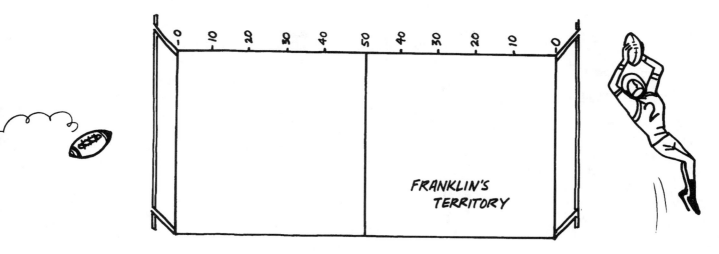

FRANKLIN'S
TERRITORY

_____ 7. Brad is over at the concession stand. He needs a hot dog, chips, and a drink; he has $3. Does Brad have enough money to buy a hot dog (a dollar and a half), a bag of chips (a half dollar), and a drink (three-quarters of a dollar)?

_____ 8. East is close to a touchdown in the first half. They have the ball $4\frac{1}{2}$ yards back from their goal line. Franklin intercepts the ball and runs $43\frac{3}{4}$ yards in the other direction. How far back from East's goal line is the ball now?

_____ 9. Bored Elizabeth, watching the clock, notices that there are 3 minutes and 50 seconds left in the third quarter ($3\frac{5}{6}$ minutes). If each quarter is 12 minutes, how much time has already passed in the third quarter?

_____ 10. Sherry ate supper at 5:20. She looks at her watch and realizes that was 3 and $\frac{1}{6}$ hours ago. What time is it now?

_____ 11. Elizabeth is so tired. She plans to be in bed in $2\frac{1}{3}$ hours. That will be 11:30 P.M. What time is it now?

_____ 12. In the last quarter, Franklin runs the ball from East's 40 yard line to a position just $6\frac{1}{3}$ yards back from their own goal line. How far do they move the ball on this play?

_____ 13. The biggest play of the game is a pass and a great run following it. James Johnston throws the ball from the 10 yard line of East. It is caught by Tom Jacobs at East's $32\frac{1}{2}$ yard line. He then runs to Franklin's $13\frac{2}{3}$ yard line. How far does the ball travel on that play?

_____ 14. Sherry and Elizabeth wait for their brother $\frac{3}{4}$ of an hour past the time when he was supposed to pick them up. If he was supposed to come at quarter past nine, when did he arrive?

Name _____

FRACTIONS IN A BACKPACK

Three friends are planning a backpacking trip to the Smoky Mountains. They can carry gear weighing up to one-fourth of their body weight. Study the information and answer the questions below:

Individual Camping Gear
sleeping bag 5 1/8 lb.
pack with frame 3 3/4 lb.
pocketknife 3/16 lb.
ground cloth 5/8 lb.
measuring drinking cup 1/8 lb.
silverware 7/16 lb.
mess kit with dip bag 15/16 lb.
full water bottle 1 1/2 lb.

Group Camping Gear
2 man tube tent 2 5/16 lb.
map 1/8 lb.
first aid kit 3 3/4 lb.
candles 7/16 lb.
camera 1 1/4 lb.
empty plastic water jug 3/8 lb.
water purification 11/16 lb.

Group Food
energy bars 1/4 lb.
2 breakfasts 7/8 lb.
2 lunches 1 3/16 lb.
2 dinners 1 5/8 lb.
hot chocolate 5/16 lb.
soups 7/16 lb.

Personal Gear
2 shirts 5/16 lb.
2 pr. pants 5/8 lb.
toiletries 1 7/8 lb.
bandanna 1/16 lb.
raincoat 1 5/16 lb.
underwear 7/8 lb.
hat 1/4 lb.
towel & washcloth 1/2 lb.
stuffed animal 11/16 lb.
reading book 7/16 lb.

Group Cooking Gear
pots & lids 2 1/8 lb.
portable grill 3/4 lb.
firestarters 1 1/16 lb.
matches 5/16 lb.
garbage bags 13/16 lb.

1. Find the total weight for each of these categories of backpacking gear.

   individual camping gear _____ group camping gear _____ group food _____

   personal gear _____ group cooking gear _____

2. The individual and personal gear weighs $19\frac{5}{8}$ pounds. Complete the chart below by subtracting each individual gear weight from her pack allowance.

Girl's name	Girl's weight	Pack allowance	Individual gear	Group share
Sally	104	26	$19\frac{5}{8}$	
Mai	101	$25\frac{1}{4}$	$19\frac{5}{8}$	
Tamika	98	$24\frac{1}{2}$	$19\frac{5}{8}$	

3. Add the group share for each of the three girls to get a total. _____

4. Total the weight of the group camping gear, group cooking gear, and group food from question 1. _____

5. Will the girls be able to carry all the group gear that they need? If yes, how much underweight is their group gear? If not, how much overweight is their group gear (subtract the answer in #4 minus the answer in #3)? _____

Name
_____

22

DANGEROUS FRACTIONS

Snow-covered mountain peaks may look beautiful, but there are dangers lurking in those peaks for hikers, climbers, and skiers. To learn about safety in the great out-of-doors, solve the fraction problems in bold type in each statement below.

_____ 1. To avoid altitude sickness on your first day of mountain climbing, don't climb above **$4499\frac{2}{5} + 4500\frac{6}{10}$ feet.**

_____ 2. To avoid windburn, you must cover **$\frac{4}{5} + \frac{3}{15}$** of your body.

_____ 3. You should be aware of not only the temperature, but also the wind chill factor. A wind speed of **$12\frac{1}{2}$ miles per hour $+ 17\frac{5}{10}$ miles per hour** can drive

_____ 5 degrees above zero to **minus $15\frac{1}{5} + 25\frac{8}{10}$ degrees.**

_____ 4. Many weather factors affect the possibility of an avalanche: temperature, wind, storms, rate of snowfall, and type of snow. For example, a sustained wind of **$19\frac{3}{4} - 4\frac{6}{8}$ miles per hour** increases the danger of an avalanche occurring.

_____ 5. Crevasses in glaciers can be extremely dangerous. One of these hidden gaps may be as deep as **$980\frac{2}{3} - 680\frac{6}{9}$ feet.**

_____ 6. We think that hypothermia can occur only when the temperature is below 0°, but it can also occur when the temperature is as warm as **$43\frac{2}{5}° + 11\frac{6}{10}°$.**

_____ 7. Snow blindness occurs when the cornea and the conjunctiva of the eye are sunburned. Generally, snow blindness does not occur until you have been out-of-doors for **$3\frac{1}{3} + 4\frac{2}{6} + 2\frac{3}{9}$ hours.**

_____ 8. When hiking in the mountains you can use an **$11\frac{3}{4} - 4\frac{2}{8}$** minute topological map. These maps have a scale of **$1\frac{3}{8} + 1\frac{4}{16}$** inches to a mile.

_____ 9. If you get lost while hiking in snow it is important to stay put. To enhance your chances of being found, tromp out a message in the snow. The letters need to be at least **$20\frac{1}{4} - 10\frac{3}{12}$ feet tall.**

_____ 10. A climber spent $2\frac{3}{4}$ hours going from point A toward point B, then found that point B was not reachable by this path, and returned to point A. The return took $1\frac{2}{3}$ hours. Then she found another route to point B, which took $3\frac{5}{6}$ hours. Altogether, how long did it take her to get from point A to point B?

Name _____

GREAT-TASTING AWARDS

Terry Castle won the Chess Master award for the Bobby Fisher League. The caterers for the awards banquet need to calculate how much food to serve the guests. There are two parts to the banquet—a reception for 160 and a luncheon for 48.

1. The reception is open to players, coaches, and parents. The proposed menu items with the amount planned per person is given below. Multiply each amount by the 160 persons expected to find the total amount of food for the caterers to order.

Food Item	Amount per person	Total amount to order
Mints	$\frac{1}{32}$ pound	_____
Pizza	$\frac{1}{8}$ pie	_____
Nuts	$\frac{3}{40}$ pound	_____
Punch	$\frac{5}{48}$ gallon	_____
Cookies	$\frac{1}{16}$ pound	_____
Fudge	$\frac{3}{64}$ pound	_____

2. The luncheon is by invitation only and includes only the top players, their parents, and one coach per club. The luncheon menu items and the budgeted amount per person are listed below. Multiply each amount by 48 to provide the caterers with the total amount which should be ordered.

Food Item	Amount per person	Total amount to order
Hotdogs	$\frac{1}{10}$ pound	_____
Hotdog buns	$\frac{1}{12}$ dozen	_____
Mustard	$\frac{1}{4}$ ounce	_____
Ketchup	$\frac{1}{3}$ ounce	_____
Hamburger	$\frac{1}{5}$ pound	_____
Hamburger buns	$\frac{1}{12}$ dozen	_____
Potato chips	$\frac{3}{16}$ pound	_____
Baked beans	$\frac{3}{8}$ cup	_____
Jello	$\frac{1}{24}$ pan	_____
Ice cream	$\frac{3}{32}$ pound	_____

3. Terry Castle's parents are so proud of him that they want all the guests from the reception to stay for lunch. Since they are willing to pay for all the extra food that will be needed, recalculate the luncheon order to accommodate 160 guests.

Name _____

THAT FISH WAS HOW BIG?

Brianna, Nan, Simon, and Jason went on a fishing trip to Lake Pardenpu. While there they decided to keep a record of the biggest fish that they could catch. Since the four friends were not going to stuff, clean, or eat what they caught, they planned to measure the length of their catch, then return them to the lake. To determine the weight of the fish that they caught they asked a state naturalist to tell them how much the big fish would weigh on average in ounces per inch.

The state naturalist gave them the following information about the fish in Lake Pardenpu.

Name of fish	Typical lengths in inches	Weight in ounces per inch
Bass, Smallmouth	15 – 25	$5\frac{15}{16}$
Bluegill Sunfish	8 – 15	$4\frac{3}{4}$
Bowfin	15 – 32	$7\frac{5}{8}$
Catfish, flathead	15 – 35	$16\frac{11}{16}$
Crappie, white	10 – 20	$3\frac{3}{8}$
Walleye	18 – 36	$8\frac{4}{5}$

For example: If Brianna caught a $10\frac{1}{2}$ inch bluegill sunfish, she would calculate its weight as $10\frac{1}{2}$ inches times $4\frac{3}{4}$ ounces per inch = $49\frac{7}{8}$ ounces.

Using the information in the chart above, calculate the weight of each fish caught.

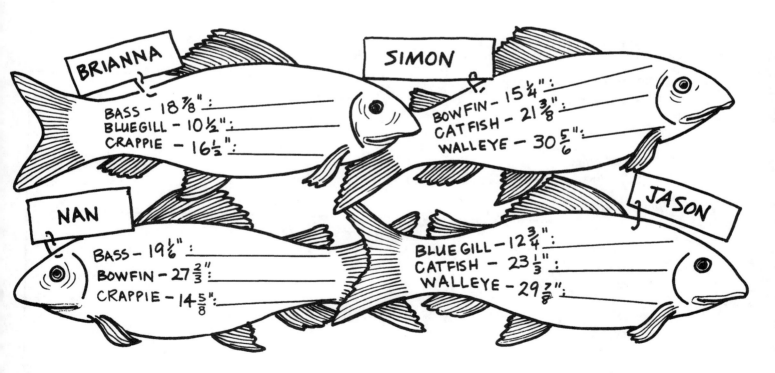

BRIANNA
BASS – $18\frac{3}{8}$″: _____
BLUEGILL – $10\frac{1}{2}$″: _____
CRAPPIE – $16\frac{1}{2}$″: _____

SIMON
BOWFIN – $15\frac{1}{4}$″: _____
CATFISH – $21\frac{3}{8}$″: _____
WALLEYE – $30\frac{5}{6}$″: _____

NAN
BASS – $19\frac{1}{6}$″: _____
BOWFIN – $27\frac{2}{3}$″: _____
CRAPPIE – $14\frac{5}{8}$″: _____

JASON
BLUEGILL – $12\frac{3}{4}$″: _____
CATFISH – $23\frac{1}{3}$″: _____
WALLEYE – $29\frac{7}{8}$″: _____

Name _____

WHAT'S COOKIN' ON THE CAMPFIRE?

A group of guys packed up for a weekend campout. They put Evan in charge of the food. He brought a recipe book that belonged to a cook at a camp. But there was a problem. The cook wrote these recipes when he was cooking in the military, so the recipes make enough food to feed an army. Reduce his recipes to the quantities listed. A group of only 10 campers will be going on the campout.

WARM YOU UP CHILI FOR 20
10 1/2 pound of hamburger
2 1/3 onions
3 1/2 green peppers
5 1/4 pound of tomatoes
6 3/4 T of chili powder
6 1/2 cans of tomato sauce
4 1/2 cans of beans

BACK WOODS POTATO SALAD FOR 30
9 1/2 lb. of potatoes
3 lb. of onions
2 1/2 lb. of celery
12 1/3 ounces of pickle relish
12 eggs
4 1/2 cups of mayonnaise
1/2 c. of mustard
2 1/2 T. of salt
1 3/4 T. of pepper
3/4 T of paprika

CRUNCHY APPLE CRISP FOR 20
12 lb. of apples
5 1/4 pound of brown sugar
8 1/3 cups of oatmeal
2 1/4 lb. of butter
2 1/2 T of cinnamon
1 3/4 t. of nutmeg

PEPPERMINT S'MORE BARS FOR 100
25 1/2 cups broken chocolate bars
55 cups crushed graham crackers
3 1/3 pounds marshmallows
3 3/4 cups crushed peppermint candy

Chili for Ten

Potato Salad for Ten

Apple Crisp for Ten

S'More's for Ten

Name

CRASHING NOT INTENDED

Stock car races are great recreational fun for car owners and spectators alike. Owners fix up old cars with hot engines and try to win money, prizes, and prestige in races. No one intends to crash these cars! But crashes do occur quite often.

Twenty cars are in this race. Which ones will crash? It will be those that have problems with incorrect answers. You'll need skills at dividing fractions to figure out which ones those are. Write "crash" beside numbers of cars that *will* crash; put a check mark (√) beside those that *will not* crash.

1. $\frac{5}{9} \div \frac{8}{15} = 1\frac{1}{24}$

2. $\frac{4}{9} \div \frac{3}{10} = 1\frac{13}{27}$

3. $\frac{5}{8} \div \frac{1}{2} = \frac{5}{16}$

4. $\frac{1}{2} \div \frac{5}{8} = \frac{1}{2}$

5. $\frac{1}{8} \div 8 = \frac{1}{64}$

6. $\frac{4}{3} \div \frac{1}{3} = \frac{4}{3}$

7. $10 \div \frac{3}{8} = 35$

8. $\frac{7}{10} \div \frac{4}{6} = 1\frac{1}{20}$

9. $8 \div \frac{3}{10} = 26\frac{2}{3}$

10. $\frac{9}{20} \div 6 = \frac{3}{40}$

11. $\frac{2}{5} \div \frac{4}{5} = \frac{1}{2}$

12. $\frac{1}{3} \div \frac{1}{3} = \frac{3}{9}$

13. $\frac{1}{2} \div \frac{1}{4} = 2$

14. $\frac{9}{27} \div \frac{1}{3} = 1$

15. $\frac{2}{3} \div \frac{7}{9} = \frac{6}{7}$

16. $\frac{4}{7} \div 4 = \frac{16}{7}$

17. $\frac{5}{9} \div \frac{1}{9} = 5$

18. $\frac{7}{9} \div \frac{9}{7} = \frac{49}{81}$

19. $\frac{1}{10} \div \frac{1}{10} = \frac{1}{100}$

20. $\frac{3}{10} \div 18 = \frac{1}{6}$

21. $\frac{6}{5} \div 1 = \frac{5}{6}$

22. $\frac{7}{8} \div \frac{6}{9} = \frac{15}{16}$

23. $\frac{1}{2} \div \frac{2}{3} = \frac{1}{6}$

24. $\frac{11}{12} \div \frac{1}{2} = 1\frac{2}{3}$

25. $\frac{1}{3} \div \frac{2}{3} = \frac{1}{2}$

26. $\frac{12}{15} \div \frac{1}{2} = 1\frac{3}{5}$

27. $\frac{1}{3} \div \frac{13}{18} = \frac{6}{13}$

28. $\frac{9}{10} \div \frac{10}{9} = \frac{81}{100}$

29. $\frac{7}{8} \div \frac{1}{4} = \frac{7}{16}$

30. $\frac{5}{25} \div \frac{1}{5} = 1$

Name

Basic Skills/Fractions & Decimals 6-8+

READ IT RIGHT!

This old-fashioned game of memory will never be a choice for inclusion in the Olympics. But it's a great game to play in order to practice any kind of math fact. This version will help you practice reading decimals correctly.

Cut out the 32 cards on this and the next page (pages 28 & 29). Mix them up well and line them up facedown in an arrangement of 8 by 5 rows. Get a partner. Take turns turning over 2 cards. If your decimal number card matches your card with the decimal number written out, you have a pair. You get to try again to locate another pair. The player with the most pairs wins. If the two cards do not form a matching pair, the cards are turned back to the facedown position, and it's your opponent's turn. To keep going and win this game, you'll have to be able to read the decimals right!

thirty-three and five hundredths	**four tenths**	**twelve hundredths**	**twenty and fifty-six thousandths**
33.05	**0.4**	**0.12**	**20.056**
three and thirty-five hundredths	**four and four tenths**	**forty-two hundredths**	**two and fourteen hundredths**
3.35	**4.4**	**0.42**	**2.14**

Use with page 29.

Name

Use with page 28.

two hundred fourteen thousandths	four hundred eighty-seven ten thousandths	thirty-three and five hundred eighty-three thousandths	forty-four hundredths
0.214	0.0487	33.583	0.44
eight thousandths	three and three hundred five thousandths	thirty-three and five hundredths	eight hundredths
0.008	3.305	33.05	0.08
four hundred eighty-seven thousandths	four hundred forty-four thousandths	four and eighty-seven hundredths	eight tenths
0.487	0.444	4.87	0.8

Name

HIGH-SPEED RECORDS

Mile runners have recorded some incredibly fast speeds—and every year, they try to break the records with faster speeds. These are some of the times for the 1 mile race recorded between the years 1973 and 1981. Rank these times from the fastest to the slowest (fastest being 1, slowest being 9).

Date	Year	Time (minutes)	Place	Rank
31 Aug.	1979	3:49.5	Crystal Palace	_____
25 July	1973	4:00.0	Motspur Park	_____
26 Aug.	1979	3:49.57	Crystal Palace	_____
17 July	1974	3:59.4	Haringey	_____
1 July	1980	3:48.82	Oslo	_____
30 June	1975	3:57.001	Stockholm	_____
20 Sept.	1978	3:52.8	Oslo	_____
26 June	1977	3:54.69	Crystal Palace	_____
28 May	1977	3:56.201	Belfast	_____

In 1912, Hannes Kolehmainen set the first 5000 meter world record with a time of 14:36.6 minutes. On the graph below, plot the points for the following times and connect them for the men's 5000 meter race.

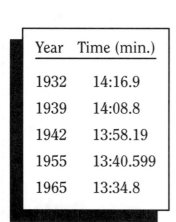

Year	Time (min.)
1932	14:16.9
1939	14:08.8
1942	13:58.19
1955	13:40.599
1965	13:34.8

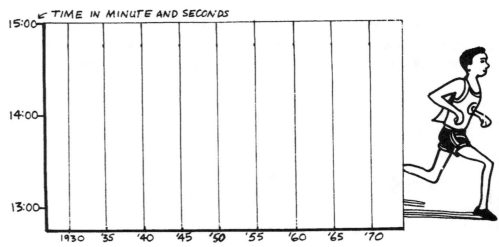

Name _____

AMAZING SPEED FACTS

You probably never timed a roller coaster, an elevator, or the hand on a wristwatch! But somebody has! Here are some surprising facts about the speed of things. The numbers are in miles per hour. Read the speeds of each of these unusual things and answer the questions about place value below each fact.

STATEMENT	SPEED (mph)

1. The tip of a ⅓ inch long hour hand on a wristwatch.
  a. What is the place-value position of the 2? _____
  b. What is the place-value position of the 7? _____
  c. What is the place-value position of the 5? _____
	0.00000275

2. The average ground speed of the three-toed sloth.
  a. What is the place-value position of the 8? _____
  b. What is the place-value position of the 9? _____
	0.098

3. A brisk walking pace for a human.
  a. What is the place-value position of the 5? _____
  b. What is the place-value position of the 7? _____
  c. What is the place-value position of the 3? _____
	3.75

4. The average speed of Roger Bannister during his 4-minute mile.
  a. What is the place-value position of the 1? _____
  b. What is the place-value position of the 5? _____
	15

5. The fastest passenger elevator. What is the place-value position of the 7? _____	**22.72**
6. The Beast roller coaster at King's Island. What is the place-value position of the 4? _____	**64.77**
7. The fastest bird in level flight, the white-throated spine-tailed swift. What is the place-value position of the 5? _____	**106.25**

8. Speed of ball in world's fastest recorded pitch
  by Nolan Ryan on August 20, 1974.
  What is the place-value position of the 9? _____
	100.9

9. The speed reached by the space shuttle Columbia on its first flight approximately 9 minutes after takeoff. What is the place-value position of the 7? _____	**16,700**
10. The speed of light. What is the place-value position of the 7? _____	**670,251,600**

Name _____

31

WELL-ROUNDED ATHLETES

Many athletes are famous for one professional sport, such as baseball, football, or basketball, but they also participate in other sports. Read about these athletes and their other famous accomplishments.

_____ 1. Terry Bradshaw (professional football player) set a high-school javelin record of 74.64 meters in 1966. Round his javelin distance to the nearest tenth.

_____ 2. Herschel Walker (professional football player) was an outstanding sprinter. He sprinted 10.10 seconds for 100 m in 1982. Round his sprint to the nearest whole number.

_____ 3. Gale Sayers (professional football player) was ranked third in the world junior long jump in 1961 with a jump of 7.58 m. Round his record to the nearest tenths place.

_____ 4. Jackie Robinson (professional baseball player) headed the world long jump ranking in 1938 with 7.78 m. Was his jump closer to 7 or 8 meters?

5. Wilt Chamberlain (professional basketball player) was a successful high jumper. His best jump was 1.99 meters. Round his record to the nearest tenth.

Round the following decimals to the underlined place-value positions.

6. 7.35 _____   7. 5.986 _____   8. 8.981 _____

9. 0.14 _____   10. 41.064 _____   11. 9.65 _____

12. 400.058 _____   13. 0.171 _____   14. 2.6543 _____

15. 17.976 _____   16. 4.993 _____   17. 0.0181 _____

18. 45.87 _____   19. 432.987 _____   20. 87.1245 _____

Name _____

TAKE TO THE SLOPES

Felipe, Raji, and Jim are taking to the ski slopes for the first time this year. Solve these problems to find out how much it costs to have fun in the snow. (Find the group's expenses.)

_____ 1. If ski boots cost $194.47, skis cost $327.28, and poles cost $65.79, how much is Felipe planning to spend if he purchases instead of rents his equipment?

_____ 2. Felipe's dad has given him $350 to spend on boots, skis, and poles. How much money will Felipe need to withdraw from his savings account to buy the equipment that he wants?

_____ 3. Raji is planning the transportation and lodging for the trip. If the round-trip airfare will be $341.93 each and three nights' stay at the motel will cost each boy $121.05, how much should each boy budget for his flight and motel room?

_____ 4. Jim is investigating renting his ski equipment. The first 2 days he is planning to ski, so he will need to rent boots for $10.87 and skis and poles for $15.46 a day. How much will his first 2 days' rental fees total?

_____ 5. The third day Jim plans to snow board. The boards rent for $8.25 an hour, and the boots rent for another $2.00 an hour. Lessons are $33.80 an hour. And he needs a lesson! He decides to snow board for 5 hours and, in that time, get a 1-hour lesson. He also must pay $35 for a lift ticket. How much will his third day on the slopes cost?

The boys plan to eat snacks at the lodge during the day to keep up their strength for skiing the slopes. Here are the prices on some typical snack foods at the lodge (tax is included).

MOUNTAIN VIEW LODGE MENU

PIZZA SLICE	$.2.73
SOFT DRINK	0.85
FRENCH FRIES	1.17
GRILLED CHEESE	1.72
BROWNIE	1.42
BAGEL	1.24
HOT CHOCOLATE	0.95

NACHOS	$ 1.06
PICKLE	0.88
COOKIES	0.95
HOT DOG	1.98
CHIPS	0.66
NOODLE SOUP	1.59
OATMEAL	1.31
SPRING WATER	1.08

_____ 6. Raji orders a pizza slice, nachos, cookies, and a soft drink. How much will his total be?
_____ If he pays with a $10 bill, how much will his change be?

_____ 7. Felipe orders hot chocolate, oatmeal, and a bagel. What does his order total and what will his change be if he pays with a $5 bill?
_____

_____ 8. Jim decides to snack on a grilled cheese sandwich with noodle soup, spring water, pickle, chips, and a brownie. What is his total food bill and what is his change from a $20 bill?
_____

Name _____

SPRINGBOARD TO DECIMALS

Melissa and Tom are on the diving team at Rocky Top School. They specialize in the 3-meter springboard competitions. Today they will be competing against Tina and John of Challenger School. Their dives will be rated on a scale of 0 to 10 by a panel of five judges. The highest and lowest scores will be deleted. The sum of the three remaining scores will be multiplied by the degree of difficulty for the dive as assigned by FINA (Federation Internationale de Natation Amateur) diving rules and upheld by United States Diving, Inc. Find the divers' final scores using the information below.

Melissa — ROCKY TOP SCHOOL

Name of dive	Scores Used 1	2	3	Sum of 3 Scores	x	Degree of Difficulty =	Final Score
Back somersault (pike position)	8.1	7.9	8.3	_____		1.8	_____
Forward 1½ somersault (tuck)	8.7	8.8	8.5	_____		1.5	_____
Inward flying somersault (pike)	7.6	7.8	7.5	_____		1.9	_____

TOTAL SCORE = _____

TOM — ROCKY TOP SCHOOL

Name of dive	Scores Used 1	2	3	Sum of 3 Scores	x	Degree of Difficulty =	Final Score
Inward dive (straight position)	7.7	7.8	8.1	_____		1.7	_____
Forward double somersault (pike)	8.4	8.6	8.9	_____		2.1	_____
Reverse 1½ somersault (tuck)	7.4	7.9	7.6	_____		2.0	_____

TOTAL SCORE = _____

John — CHALLENGER SCHOOL

Dive name	Sum of 3 Scores	Degree of Difficulty	Final Score
Back double somersault (tuck)	22.6	2.0	_____
Inward Flying somersault (pike)	24.7	1.9	_____
Forward triple somersault (tuck)	21.9	2.5	_____

TOTAL SCORE = _____

Tina — CHALLENGER SCHOOL

Dive name	Sum of 3 Scores	Degree of Difficulty	Final Score
Reverse flying somersault (tuck)	23.4	1.8	_____
Forward double somersault (pike)	21.1	2.1	_____
Inward double somersault (pike)	22.8	2.6	_____

TOTAL SCORE = _____

Who had the highest final score? _____

Name _____

THREE TIMES THE WORK

Mitch and Debbie are preparing to compete in a triathlon. Participants are required to swim, bike, and run. It is considered a grueling test of fitness. Mitch has been jogging and Debbie has been swimming to stay in shape, but they have decided to train in all three events to prepare for the Cherokee Triathlon. Answer these questions about their training. (Remember: rate x time = distance; distance ÷ time = rate; and distance ÷ rate = time.) Round to the nearest hundred.

1. For their training ride, Debbie and Mitch decided to cycle the 12.8 mile course at the City Park. Calculate their rates in miles per hour. (First, change minutes to hours by dividing the minute time by 60. Then divide the distance by the time to find the rate.)

	Time	Time in Hours	Distance	=	Rate (mph)
a. Debbie	26.4 min.	_____	12.8 mi.		_____
b. Mitch	25.7 min.	_____	12.8 mi.		_____

2. Next they went to the pool to check on their swimming rates. They decided to swim 2000 m. (Change meters to miles by dividing by 1609.76.)

	Time	Time in Hours	Distance	=	Rate (mph)
a. Debbie	25.1 min.	_____	_____ mi.		_____
b. Mitch	26.9 min.	_____	_____ mi.		_____

3. The mini-marathon course in their city measures 13.4 miles. Calculate the rates for their running of this course based on their times.

	Time	Time in Hours	Distance	=	Rate (mph)
a. Debbie	66.4 min.	_____	13.4 mi.		_____
b. Mitch	59.8 min.	_____	13.4 mi.		_____

4. On the day of the big race Debbie and Mitch had calculated the rates that they needed to maintain in order to have what they felt was a respectable showing for their first triathlon. Based on their rates, calculate what their time goals will be in each of the three events. (Recall: Distance / Rate = Time)

Debbie's		Distance (mi.)	/	Rate (mph)	=	Time (hr.)
a.	Swim	2.4		14.7		_____
	Cycle	112.0		26.4		_____
	Run	26.2		9.9		_____

Mitch's		Distance (mi.)	/	Rate (mph)	=	Time (hr.)
b.	Swim	2.4		15.3		_____
	Cycle	112.0		24.8		_____
	Run	26.2		11.6		_____

Name _____

FACE OFF!

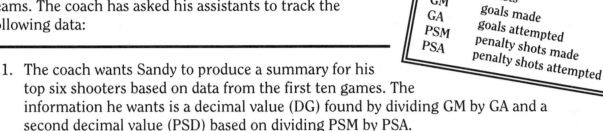

Initials	Meaning
G	games played
R	rebounds
P	total points
A	assists
GM	goals made
GA	goals attempted
PSM	penalty shots made
PSA	penalty shots attempted

Sandy Slapshot has been asked by the coach to update the statistics on the girls' and boys' Slippery Springs ice hockey teams. The coach has asked his assistants to track the following data:

1. The coach wants Sandy to produce a summary for his top six shooters based on data from the first ten games. The information he wants is a decimal value (DG) found by dividing GM by GA and a second decimal value (PSD) based on dividing PSM by PSA.

   Example: Sal Valenko had 14 goals made (GM) in 42 goals attempted (GA). So Sal's DG would be $14/42 = 0.333$; Sal's PSM = 3 and his PSA = 12, so his PSD = $3/12 = 0.250$.

Name	*GM/GA*	*DG*	*PSM/PSA*	*PSD*
Sal Valenko	$14/42$	0.333	$3/12$	0.250
Tseno Inqvest	$15/40$	_____	$6/14$	_____
Jeb Diskov	$18/45$	_____	$9/32$	_____
Tina Beaufort	$11/55$	_____	$7/30$	_____
Niki Tyler	$12/72$	_____	$5/26$	_____
Michelle Guilford	$13/52$	_____	$3/27$	_____

2. The coach would also like to know the following statistics on a per game basis: rebounds per game (R/G), total points per game (P/G), and assists per game (A/G). (Note: Total points are found by adding together goals made, penalty shots made, and assists.)

Name	G	R	P	A	R/G	P/G	A/G
S. Valenko	10	17	33	11	____	____	____
T. Inqvest	9	14	30	9	____	____	____
J. Diskov	10	11	39	12	____	____	____
T. Beaufort	9	9	25	8	____	____	____
N. Tyler	10	12	30	13	____	____	____
M. Guilford	9	13	26	10	____	____	____

3. Billy "the Puckman" Johnson is the team's starting goalie. In the 10 games he has played, he was able to stop 149 shots on goal, while allowing 38 goals to be scored. Calculate the following two statistics on Billy the Puckman.

   Saves per game = $149/10 = $ _____ (decimal value)

   Goals allowed per game = $38/10 = $ _____ (decimal value)

Name

36

A BOXING LEGEND SPEAKS

Muhammad Ali (formerly known as Cassius Clay) is considered by many to be the greatest heavyweight boxing champion of all time. He first came to prominence at the 1960 Rome Summer Olympics when he won a gold medal in boxing. You may have seen him lighting the flame at the opening ceremonies for the 1996 Summer Olympics in Atlanta.

The following is a famous quote by Muhammad Ali that refers to his boxing style. Change the decimals to fractions to reveal the letters in the quote.

____	____	____	____	____	____	____	____	____	____
0.105	0.55	0.75	0.08	0.555	0.55	0.38	0.15	0.625	0.08

____	____	____	____	____	____	____	____	____
0.972	0.425	0.555	0.555	0.625	0.58	0.105	0.55	0.3

____	____	____	____	____	____	____	____	____
0.548	0.555	0.38	0.4	0.855	0.55	0.38	0.15	0.625

____	____	____	____
0.08	0.972	0.625	0.625

I'm the greatest!!

ALPHABET OF FRACTIONS FOR DECIPHERING

A	2/25	H	31/40	O	3/4	V	4/5
B	243/250	I	19/50	P	147/200	W	49/50
C	9/40	J	57/200	Q	13/40	X	149/200
D	1/5	K	3/20	R	29/50	Y	3/10
E	5/8	L	11/20	S	137/250	Z	3/50
F	21/200	M	203/250	T	111/200		
G	171/200	N	2/5	U	17/40		

Name _____

BIRDS THAT COUNT

Marcia and Bradley helped with the Audubon Society's bird-counting project. They volunteered to be on a team that made the semiannual count of birds at the Municipal Park. After returning to the park shelter a tabulation was made of all the birds that were sighted and the following statistics were compiled.

Example: Of the 1240 total birds sighted, 36 were cardinals. $^{36}/_{1240} = .029 = 2.9\%$

1. The decimal values in the chart below were found by dividing the count by 1240 which represents the total birds sighted this year. Find the equivalent percent of each.

Name of bird	Count	Decimal Value	Percent
a. Starling	556	0.448	_____
b. Grackle	97	0.078	_____
c. Cardinal	36	0.029	2.9%
d. Bluebird	11	0.009	_____
e. Wren	74	0.060	_____
f. Chickadee	68	0.055	_____
g. Sparrow	53	0.043	_____
h. Finch	81	0.065	_____
i. Woodpecker	51	0.041	_____
j. Catbird	20	0.016	_____
k. Mockingbird	35	0.028	_____
l. Other birds	158	0.128	_____

2. The chart below shows the counts from this year and last year, and the percent change that occurred for each category. Use the percent change to find an equivalent decimal value.

Name of bird	Count this year	Count last year	Percent change	Decimal value
a. Starling	556	524	6.1%	0.061
b. Grackle	97	84	15.5%	_____
c. Cardinal	36	42	14.3%	_____
d. Bluebird	11	50	78.0%	_____
e. Wren	74	82	9.8%	_____
f. Chickadee	68	75	9.3%	_____
g. Sparrow	53	66	19.7%	_____
h. Finch	81	78	3.8%	_____
i. Woodpecker	51	71	28.2%	_____
j. Catbird	20	39	48.7%	_____
k. Mockingbird	35	47	25.5%	_____
l. Other birds	158	103	53.4%	_____

Name

MUSICAL STATISTICS

Mario is curious about the types of music played by the top radio stations in his area. He has gotten together with some friends and started keeping track of music played. He wants his final statistics to be in the form of percentages, but he has been keeping track of his counts in the form of fractions. Use the charts to change his statistics into percentages.

1. In his first count, he listened to a popular radio station for one hour and counted twenty-five songs categorizing them by decade or as a current Top 40 Hit.

Category of song	Fraction (over 25)	Fraction (over 100)	Decimal	Percent
a. Decade - 50s, 60s	2/25	8/100	0.08	8%
b. Decade - 70s	4/25	_____	_____	_____
c. Decade - 80s	7/25	_____	_____	_____
d. Decade - 90s	3/25	_____	_____	_____
e. Current Top 40	9/25	_____	_____	_____

2. In a thirty-minute period he surfed as many stations as he could and counted fifty songs, arranging the count by category.

Music by category	Fraction (over 50)	Fraction (over 100)	Decimal	Percent
a. Pop/Rock	14/50	28/100	0.28	28%
b. Country	11/50	_____	_____	_____
c. R&B/Rap	9/50	_____	_____	_____
d. Christian	7/50	_____	_____	_____
e. Oldies	6/50	_____	_____	_____
f. Classical	3/50	_____	_____	_____

FREAKY FERGUS — DISC JOCKEY
K-NOIZ — 940 FM

Name

OFF THE TEE

Martina is going to play a round of golf at the Falling Waters Golf Course. She has heard that this new eighteen-hole course is one of the most unusual and challenging courses around. She and her friends will need a lot of golfing skill to do well on this course. You'll need to be skilled at changing fractions into percents to solve these golf problems.

_____ 1. The fees for the course and golf cart come to $159. Martina's share comes to $61. Change $^{61}/_{159}$ to a percent to find what percent of the fees she paid.

2. On the first hole Martina's score was an eight, which included two penalty strokes and three puts.
_____ a. Change $^2/_8$ to a percent to see what percent of her strokes were due to penalties.
_____ b. Change $^3/_8$ to a percent to see what percent of her strokes were puts.

3. Of the eighteen holes, three are par threes, five are par fives, and ten are par fours. What percent of the holes are:
_____ a. par threes?
_____ b. par fours?
_____ c. par fives?

_____ 4. Martina and her friends buy 40 golf tees for driving the golf balls. If Martina takes 12 of the tees, what percent of them should she pay for?

_____ 5. After playing nine holes, the golfing partners go into the clubhouse to eat a quick lunch. Martina's food and drink come to $7, and the total bill is $32. What percent of the lunch bill is Martina's?

6. To determine how long it takes to play each hole, Martina notices that par threes take 10 minutes to play, par fours take 12 minutes to play, and par fives take 15 minutes to play. If the total playing time of the eighteen holes is 225 minutes, then find what percent of golfing time is spent playing each.
_____ a. par three?
_____ b. par four?
_____ c. par five?

7. At the end of the round, Martina reflects on her score of 97 strokes. She adds up her strokes by category to see that she used 36 puts, 15 shots with woods, 20 iron shots, and 26 shots using wedges. Find the percent of her total score that can be attributed to:
_____ a. puts
_____ b. shots using woods
_____ c. iron shots
_____ d. shots using wedges

Name

CAN YOU CANOE?

Three friends have gone on a four-day canoe trip that will take them 42 miles down the Buffalo River. They have practiced their canoeing skills and boating safety on the lake and are ready to tackle a new challenge.

1. A normal 12-hour camping day consists of: 1 hour for breakfast and cleanup, 1 hour to load the canoes and take down the tents, 3 hours of morning paddling, 1 hour for swim break and lunch, 3 hours of afternoon paddling, 1 hour to unload canoes and set up camp, 2 hours for firebuilding, dinner, and cleanup.

    _____ a. What percent of the day is used for canoeing?

    _____ b. What percent of the day is used to swim and to prepare, eat, and clean up from meals?

    _____ c. What percent of the day is used to load and unload canoes and set up and take down the camp?

2. Their plan calls for the following miles to be canoed each day: day one 6 miles, day two 12 miles, day three 16 miles, and day four 8 miles.

    _____ a. What percent of the trip will be covered on the last day?

    _____ b. The first and second day taken together represent what portion of the trip?

    _____ c. Day three covers the most miles. What percent of the trip does this represent?

3. Sheila, Jamie, and Tony will be sharing a canoe. Each one will take turns bowing (paddling in the front of the boat), sterning (paddling and steering from the rear, and duffing (sitting in the middle resting). The chart below represents how many miles each paddler spent in each position in the canoe.

	Bowing	Sterning	Duffing
Sheila	10	18	14
Jamie	15	15	12
Tony	17	9	16

_____ a. Who spent the largest portion of the trip in the bow?

_____ What percent of his or her trip did this paddler spend in the bow?

_____ b. Who spent the least amount of time duffing?

_____ What percent of his or her trip was spent resting in the middle of the boat?

_____ c. Who spent the most time sterning?

_____ What percent of the trip did he or she spend steering the canoe?

_____ d. Who paddled the most (spent the most miles bowing and sterning)?

_____ What percent of the trip did he or she spend paddling?

Name _____

LOST: SOFTBALL STATS

Marlene is the manager of the Marvelous Mavens softball team. She has kept the statistics for the team throughout the season. Each page in her team notebook has been dedicated to a different type of softball statistic, but the page of TOTALS has slipped out. Help her to recreate this page in time for the team's end-of-the-season banquet and awards ceremony.

_____ 1. Jose's leading batting percentage is 43.23%. If he had 162 at-bats, how many times did he get a hit?

_____ 2. The Mavens' winning percentage was 55%. If they played 41 games in all, how many did they win?

_____ 3. Ralph, the Mavens' best pitcher, won 75% of the games that he pitched. If he pitched 11 games, how many did he win?

_____ 4. Tim, the shortest player on the team, walked the most number of times. If Tim came to bat 155 times and walked 11% of the these times, find the number of walks issued to Tim by opposing pitchers.

_____ 5. Solon is the team's top base stealer. 23% of the time he gets on base he gets a stolen base. If Solon got on base 76 times, how many times did he steal a base?

_____ 6. Ken is the most accurate pitcher on the team. 68% of his pitches are strikes. If the coach usually lets him pitch about 90 pitches per game, how many strikes does he throw per game?

_____ 7. Jonathan has the best slugging percentage of all the Mavens with 59%. (Slugging percentage is found by comparing total bases to total at bats.) If Jonathan had 124 at bats, how many total bases did he get this season?

_____ 8. Mitchell is the Mavens' home run king. He was able to hit a homer 8% of the time he was at bat. If Mitchell had 152 at bats, how many home runs did he hit?

_____ 9. Scott is the pitching staff's saves leader saving 72% of the games in which he pitched. If he pitched in 28 games, how many saves did he earn?

_____ 10. Josh is the Mavens' catcher. He threw to second base 137 times trying to catch base stealers. He was successful in cutting down 41% of the runners he attempted to throw out. How many opposing runners did he throw out at second?

Name _____

ON TO WIMBLEDON?

Jana and Cindy have been playing tennis in the hopes of making the high school team in the spring. Their most recent head to head match was won by Jana in three sets with scores of 6–1, 2–6, and 6–3. Here are the statistics of their most recent match. They each might learn something to improve their games if they examine these numbers carefully. You will need to write a ratio to analyze each statistic.

1. Since Jana's games won are listed first in the set scores, she won 14 of the 24 games that were played.

   _____ a. Write Jana's wins to total games played as a reduced ratio.

   _____ b. Find a reduced ratio for Jana's games won to Cindy's games won.

_____ 2. In the first set Jana served 36 points and got 16 first serves in bounds. State her first serves to points served as a reduced ratio.

_____ 3. Jana won 12 of the points in which she got her first serve in bounds. Write a reduced ratio to show these points compared to her first 16 good serves.

_____ 4. Jana served two aces (service winners) out of the 16 first serves that were good. Find a reduced ratio for Jana's service aces to good first serves.

The chart below gives an analysis of Cindy's shots for the match.

TYPE OF SHOT	WINNERS	GOOD SHOTS	UN-FORCED ERRORS	TOTAL
SERVES	12	32	44	88
GROUND STROKES	75	49	41	165
LOBS	8	10	4	22
VOLLEYS	9	3	12	24
OVERHEADS	2	4	10	16
TOTAL	106	98	111	315

5. Find reduced ratios for each of the following comparisons.

   _____ a. unforced errors that were volleys to total volleys

   _____ b. lobs that were good shots to lobs that were unforced errors

   _____ c. total overheads to overhead shots that were unforced errors

   _____ d. good shots that were ground strokes to total good shots

Name _____

AND THEY'RE OFF!

Sam is a runner. He can run the 1000 meters in 2.50 minutes. That is a ratio of 1000:2.50 or 4000:10 or 400:1 and can be stated as a rate of 400 meters per minute. Sam is interested in investigating the speeds achieved in other races.

1. The Kentucky Derby is a famous horse race in Louisville, Kentucky, that covers a distance of 1 mile 550 yards or 2110 meters. One horse ran the race in 2 minutes.

_____ a. Find the rate achieved by the race horse in meters per minute.

_____ b. Since 2 minutes is 120 seconds, find the rate of the race horse in meters per second.

_____ 2. Amy Van Dyken swam to a new American record in the 50 m freestyle at the 1996 Atlanta Olympic Games with a time of just under 25 seconds. Find her rate in meters per second.

_____ 3. Amateur cyclists racing from a standing start can cover 1000 meters in 62.5 seconds. Find the rate of these cyclists in meters per second.

4. Twelve dogs can pull a sled through the snow a distance of 3900 meters every 10 minutes.

_____ a. Give the sled dog's speed in meters per minute.

_____ b. Since 10 minutes is 600 seconds, find the dog's speed in meters per second.

5. Racing greyhounds can achieve speeds over 37 miles per hour. 37 miles is about 60,000 meters, and one hour is 3600 seconds.

_____ a. Calculate the greyhound's speed in meters per second.

_____ b. According to their speeds in m/s, which is faster: the horse in #1, the cyclist in #3, or the greyhound?

_____ 6. At the Barcelona Olympics the U.S. Men's 4 x 100 relay team of Marsh, Burrell, Mitchell, and Lewis covered the 400 meters in 37.4 seconds. Give this speed in m/s.

_____ 7. Dale Jarrett won the pole position for the Daytona 500 in 1995 with a speed of 193.5 mph. This is equivalent to 309,600 meters per 3600 seconds. What is this speed in meters per second?

_____ 8. The fastest Indianapolis 500 was won in 1990 by Arie Luyendyk when his car covered the 500 miles in 2.69 hours. Give this winning speed in miles per hour.

_____ 9. Kenny Bernstein set the Top Fuel Drag Racing speed in 1994 when his car covered the 1320 foot strip in 2.86 seconds. Find this speed in feet per second.

Name _____

ARE WE LOST—OR WHAT?

Irma and Ima are going to participate in their second State Orienteering Meet. It is a 2-person novice team event to be held in the state park. Both girls are confident of their compass skills and are anxious to try out their map reading under competitive conditions. They will pick up their control card and map to begin at 9:05 A.M. The map is drawn using a scale of 1 cm = 50 m. Let's hope they don't get lost. Let's hope you remember how to solve proportions. You'll need to write and solve proportions for several of these problems.

SHOULD WE TAKE THE DETOUR ?

_____ 1. Irma begins by measuring the distance between the start triangle and the circle on the first control point while Ima sets the compass to a bearing of 325°. Since the distance on the map is 7 cm, the competitors set up a proportion to calculate the actual distance to the first control point. Write the proportion and solve it to find the distance to the first control point. (You'll need to use cross multiplication.)

2. The most direct route from the first to second control points is a train trestle, but it has been marked out of bounds. Ima and Irma have measured and calculated the distances of two alternate paths, but must determine which one is the quicker route.

_____ a. One path follows a winding fire road for 750 m. If 50 m of fire road takes 24 seconds to travel, how long will this route take?

_____ b. The second route is 320 m and requires crossing a hilly forest and a stream. If the girls can cover about 40 m in 48 seconds, how long will this take?

_____ c. Which was faster?

3. Irma notices that the process of taking six compass bearings has taken a total of 96 seconds.

_____ a. Solve the proportion $\frac{2}{?} = \frac{6}{96}$ to find out how long 2 compass bearings take.

_____ b. How long will it take to complete 5 compass bearings?

4. The competitors have to decide whether to go right or left around an irregularly shaped field that says, "NO TRESPASSING." While the distance to the left will take 240 seconds to travel, it will require stopping to take 5 compass bearings. The distance around the right side will take 290 seconds but will require 2 compass bearings.

_____ a. How long will it take to go right?

_____ b. How long will it take to go left?

_____ c. Which is quicker according to your calculations, and by how many seconds?

_____ 5. The home leg shows a bearing of 120° to get to the two concentric circles marking the finish area. If the final leg is 375 m, how long is the line on the map marking the home leg?

_____ 6. The total time for Irma and Ima was 42 minutes. Last year they finished in 16th place with a time of 48 minutes. The ratio of their place to their total time is the same as last year's ratio of place to total time. What will their finishing place be this year?

Name _____

UNDERGROUND EXPLORATIONS

Maria and six certified spelunking friends are going to explore Salamander Cave to collect samples for environmental testing. It has been reported that sewage thrown into sinkholes has polluted the underground stream which feeds the cave. The strenuous trip will take seven hours and will involve rope work for climbing and rappelling. Use proportions to solve these problems. Write the answers.

1. To get the exploration party from the cars to the mouth (entrance) of the cave involves following a map which has a scale of 3 cm to 1000 ft.

   a. The map shows that the distance from the road to the spring in the forest is a distance of 11 cm. Write a proportion to calculate the distance to the spring in feet. _____

   b. The distance from the spring to the cave is about 2500 ft. Write a proportion that will calculate how far apart the spring and the cave should be on the map. _____

2. Two lengths of rope will be necessary equipment for this excursion. One rope will be 350 ft. long to rappel into the cave and another rope will be used for scaling rock face. The specialty climbing rope being used weighs 2 lbs. for every 15 ft.

   a. Write a proportion to calculate the weight of the 350-ft. rope. _____

   b. If the second rope weighs 48 lbs., write a proportion to calculate its length. _____

3. To get into the cave, the spelunkers will rappel down a 315-ft. pit. This requires the use of carabiners on a rack so that the descent can be controlled. For each 75 lbs. of weight one carabiner is placed on the rack. Write a proportion to calculate how many carabiners are necessary to equip a rappeller that weighs 200 lbs. with his equipment. _____

4. The certified climber will scale an 85-ft. rock face. For safety he will install spring-loaded camming devices into creases in the rock every 15 ft., which will break his fall in the event that he should slip. Write a proportion that will help to calculate the number of spring-loaded camming devices necessary to make a safe climb.

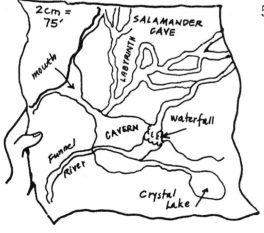

5. The cave map is drawn to the scale of 2 cm = 75 ft.

   a. If the map shows the waterfall to be 9 cm from the mouth of the cave, write a proportion that will calculate how far into the cave the party must hike before reaching the waterfall.

   _____

   b. If the back of the cave is known to be 1200 ft. from the mouth of the cave, write a proportion to figure how many centimeters in length that the map of the cave should be.

   _____

Name _____

6. Every spelunker is responsible for bringing three sources of light that will each burn twice as long as the expected duration of the trip underground. Maria has chosen to bring a battery-operated headlamp, chemical light sticks, and candles. Since the trip is to last 7 hours, each of her light sources should burn 14 hours. Write a proportion to calculate the number of light sticks each spelunker would need to bring if each light stick lasts 4 hours. _____

7. When the explorers reach the back of the cave, they will take water samples from Crystal Lake to test for pollution. The last time the lake water was tested it was determined that the lake contained no coliform bacteria.

   a. If a 1000 ml sample contains 0.1 ml of coliform pollution, write a proportion to calculate the gallons of coliform pollution in a 500,000-gallon lake. _____

   b. If 3 parts per million is the standard for water that can be made safe by boiling, write a proportion for calculating how many milliliters of coliform pollution must be found in a 1000 ml sample in order to declare Crystal Lake too polluted for drinking. _____

8. To climb out of the pit at the mouth of the cave, Maria has chosen to use prussic knots. If each turn in the knot is capable of handling 50 lbs. of weight, write a proportion to determine how many turns Maria should tie into each of her prussic knots if she estimates that her total weight will be 160 lbs. with clothing, equipment, and mud as she prepares to make her ascent out of the cave. _____

9. The girls spent 5 minutes climbing for every 2 minutes they were involved in other exploring tasks. If they were in the cave for 420 minutes, how much of that time did they spend climbing? (Set up a proportion to help solve this.) _____

10. Ima can carry 8 pounds of equipment for each 30 lbs. of her body weight. If she is carrying 30.4 lbs., how much does she weigh? (Set up a proportion to help solve this.) _____

Name _____

HIGHS & LOWS

Skydivers and scuba divers share diving thrills—but at opposite extremes of location. Use their places, high in the sky or deep down under the ocean, for fun in this exercise. Examine each problem below. (The answers are given!) If the answer is correct, write the number of the problem in the box high in the sky. If the answer is wrong, write the number way down below near the scuba diver.

1. $13/52 \approx 1/3$

2. $6\frac{2}{3} + 9\frac{4}{7} = 16\frac{1}{4}$

3. $3.66 = .0366\%$

4. $8/11 = 0.727$

5. In $12/18 = x/126$, $x = 84$

6. 15% of $8400 = 1200$

7. $15/40 = 37.5\%$

8. $7/9 \times 4/5 = 28/45$

9. $7/2 = 4/2 = 5\frac{1}{2}$

10. $0.89 = 8.9\%$

11. $9/7 \approx 12/10$

12. $0.428 = 3/7$

13. $60.32 + 9.9 = 70.31$

14. 55% of $212 = 116.6$

15. $147/49 = 3$

16. $4\frac{1}{2} \times 3\frac{1}{3} = 15$

17. 80% of $95 = 76$

18. $2.33 \times 6.11 = 14.44$

19. $9/10 \div 3/5 = 1\frac{1}{5}$

20. $1.06 \div 1.06 = 2.12$

21. $\frac{1}{2} \div \frac{1}{8} = \frac{1}{16}$

22. $7/10 \div 2/4 = 1\frac{1}{5}$

23. $8\frac{1}{3} - 7\frac{5}{6} = \frac{1}{2}$

24. $8/9 = 93\%$

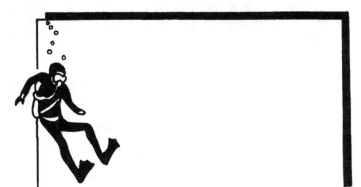

Name

A MATTER OF SECONDS

In sporting events such as running, seconds—even fractions of seconds—make all the difference. Races are won or lost by tenths, hundredths, or thousandths of seconds. So decimals really matter. Here are some facts about winning times in the 1996 Summer Olympic Games. Use these facts to answer the questions below.

Donovan Bailey of Canada won the men's 100-meter race in 9.84 seconds.
Gail Devers of the U.S. won the women's 100-meter race in 10.94 seconds.
Michael Johnson of the U.S. won the men's 200-meter race in 19.32 seconds.
Marie-Jose Perec of France won the women's 200-meter race in 22.12 seconds.
Michael Johnson of the U.S. won the men's 400-meter race in 43.49 seconds.
Marie-Jose Perec of France won the women's 400-meter race in 48.25 seconds.
The Canadian team won the men's 400-meter relay race in 37.69 seconds.
The U.S. team won the women's 400-meter relay race in 41.95 seconds.
Allen Johnson of the U.S. won the men's 110-meter hurdle race in 12.95 seconds.
Ludmila Enquist of Sweden won the women's 100-meter hurdle race in 12.58 seconds.
Derrick Adkins of the U.S. won the men's 400-meter hurdle race in 47.95 seconds.
Deon Hemmings of Jamaica won the women's 400-meter hurdle race in 52.82 seconds.

_____ 1. What is the difference between the winning time of the men's and women's 400-m hurdles?

_____ 2. How much longer did Michael Johnson run for the 400 m than the 200 m?

_____ 3. How much longer did it take Ludmila to run the 100-m hurdles than it took Gail Devers to run the 100-m race?

_____ 4. How long did all the hurdlers run, total?

_____ 5. How much faster was the Canadian men's relay team than the U.S. women's relay team?

_____ 6. How much shorter was Donovan Bailey's run than Derrick Adkins' hurdle race?

_____ 7. How much longer did the slowest hurdle race take than the fastest?

_____ 8. How much faster did Marie-Jose run the 200 m than the 400 m?

_____ 9. Find the difference between the fastest of all the 400-m races and the slowest.

_____ 10. How long did all the women run, total?

Name _____

MORE TOP 10 QUESTIONS

_____ 1. Of the Top 10 Olympic Gold Medal winners of all time, 4 are U.S. athletes: Ray Ewry with 10 medals, Mark Spitz with 9, Carl Lewis with 8, and Matt Biondi with 8. Of these medals, what percentage was won by Carl Lewis?

_____ 2. Top 10 run-scoring baseball players Babe Ruth and Hank Aaron both scored 2174 runs in regular games in their careers. Ty Cobb, #1, scored 2245. Write a decimal showing the comparison of Cobb's total to Hank's and Babe's.

_____ 3. The Top 10 largest major ballparks have a total capacity of 586,252 seats. The Seattle Mariner's Kingdome holds 59,166. What percentage is this of the total capacity?

_____ 4. Of the Top 10 wage earners in the National Basketball Association in 1995–1996, Patrick Ewing is # 1 with $18,700,000. Grant Hill, #10, earned $4,000,000. Write a reduced ratio showing the comparison of Hill's income to Ewing's.

_____ 5. Secretariat is at the top of the Top 10 list of Kentucky Derby winners with a winning time, in 1973, of 1 minute 59.4 seconds. Number 10, Bold Forbes, won in 1976 in 2 minutes, 1.6 seconds. What is the difference between their times?

_____ 6. Juan Fangio is the oldest of the Top 10 oldest World Champion automobile racers. His age at the time of his win is 1.32 times older than Albert Ascari, #10. Ascari was 35. How old was Fangio when he won his title?

_____ 7. 277,004 points were scored in the regular season by 1996 by basketball's Top 10 NBA career-scorers. Kareem Abdul-Jabbar, #1 on the list, scored 38,387 of those points. What percentage of the total points are his?

_____ 8. Willie Shoemaker had the most wins of any U.S. jockey. Sandy Hawley, who is #10 on the Top 10 list, had approximately 6200 wins, which was 70% of the number of Willie's wins. Approximately how many wins did Willie have?

_____ 9. Nancy Green of Canada has won 0.07% of the women's alpine ski World Cup titles of the total held by the Top 10 women. The total is 29. How many has Nancy won?

_____ 10. Walking is first on the list of the Top 10 sports activities people choose in the U.S. 71 million people participate in this activity. Pool (billiards) is #8 on the list, with 48% as many participants as those walking. How many people said they were pool players?

Name _____

APPENDIX

CONTENTS

Glossary 53

Fractions & Decimals Skills Test 56

Skills Test Answer Key 59

Answers 60

Basic Skills/Fractions & Decimals 6-8+

GLOSSARY OF TERMS RELATED TO FRACTIONS & DECIMALS

Associative Property—a property stating that changing the grouping of numbers does not change the sum or product
Ex: (3.4 + 6.2) + 1.1 = 3.4 + (6.2 + 1.1)

common denominator—a common multiple of two or more denominators
Ex: The fractions ¾ and ¼ have a common denominator.

common factor—a number that is a factor of two or more numbers
Ex: 3 is a factor common to 3, 6, and 9.

common multiple—a number that is a multiple of two or more numbers
Ex: 12 is a common multiple of 2, 3, 4, and 6.

Commutative Property—a property stating that changing the order of the numbers does not change the sum or product
Ex: 3 x 6 = 6 x 3.

composite number—any whole number that has more than two factors (36 is a composite number because it has 1 and 36 as factors plus several other factors: 2, 3, 4, 6, 9, 12)

cross multiplication—a process for solving proportions where the numerator of one fraction is multiplied with the denominator of a second fraction and that product is compared with the product that comes from multiplying the denominator of that first fraction with the numerator of the second. This is also a way to see if fractions are equivalent. In equivalent fractions, cross multiplication yields the same product.

cross products—products used to check if two fractions are equivalent
Ex: ⅔ = ⁴⁄₆ because their cross products are equal (2 x 6 = 3 x 4).

decimal numeral—a name for a fractional number expressed with a decimal point
Ex: 0.56 (meaning 56 hundredths); 3.14 is a *mixed* decimal numeral.

decimal system—a numeration system based on grouping by tens

denominator—the bottom number in a fraction
Ex: 6 is the denominator in the fraction ⅙.

divisible—capable of being divided evenly without a remainder
Ex: 42 is divisible by 1, 2, 3, 6, 7, 14, 21, and 42.

equation—a number sentence which states that two numbers or quantities are equal
Ex: 4.0 x 3.1 = 12.4.

estimate—an answer that is not exact

even numbers—numbers that are multiples of 2
Ex: 2, 4, 6, 8, 10, etc.

factor—any of two or more numbers that are multiplied to obtain a product
Ex: 6 and 8 are factors of 48 because 6 x 8 gives a product of 48.

fraction—a number in the form of a/b where b is not zero, that compares part of an object or set to the whole object or set
Ex: $6/7$ is a fraction.

greatest common factor—the greatest of the common factors of two or more numbers
Ex: 12 is the greatest common factor of 12, 24, and 36.

Identity Property for Addition—property stating that the sum of 0 and any number is that number
Ex: $0 + 4 = 4$ and $7 + 0 = 7$

Identity Property for Multiplication—property stating that the product of 1 and any number is that number
Ex: $5 \times 1 = 5$ and $1 \times 25 = 25$

inequality—a number sentence that states two numbers or quantities are not equal
Ex: $4 + 6 + 7 \neq 15$

least common denominator—the least common multiple of two or more denominators
Ex: In the fractions $3/4$, $1/3$, and $4/5$, 60 is the least common multiple of 4, 3, and 5. Therefore 60 is the least common denominator for the fractions.

least common multiple—the least or smallest of the common multiples of two or more numbers
Ex: The numbers 2, 5, and 4 have 20, 40, and 60 as some of their common multiples. But 20 is the smallest of these. Therefore, 20 is the least common multiple for these three numbers.

lowest terms—a fraction is in lowest terms if the greatest common factor of the numerator and denominator is 1
Ex: the lowest common denominator for 5 and 7 is 1;
the fraction $5/7$ is in lowest terms.

mixed number—a number that has a whole number part and a fractional number part. Mixed numbers can be mixed fractions or mixed decimals.

mixed decimal number—a number that has a whole number part and a decimal part
Ex: 579.034

mixed fractional number—a number that has a whole number part and a fraction part
Ex: $44 6/7$

multiple—the product of a given number and any whole number
Ex: 4, 6, 8, 10, and 12 are all multiples of the number 2.

Name

number sentence—a sentence showing a relationship among numbers
 Ex: $4/5 + 2/3 = 17/15$

numerator—the top number in a fraction
 Ex: In the fraction $11/14$, 11 is the numerator.

odd numbers—numbers that are not multiples of 2
 Ex: 3, 5, 7, 9 are odd numbers.

percent—the ratio of a number to 100, expressed using the % symbol
 Ex: 46% is a comparison of 46 to 100.

percentage—a part of a total amount

prime factors—factors of a given number that are prime numbers
 Ex: Of the factors of the number 36, the factors 2 and 3 are prime factors.

prime number—a number that has exactly two factors, 1 and itself
 Ex: 3 is a prime number.

product—the answer in a multiplication problem

proportion—an equation which states that two ratios are equal
 Ex: $4/7 = 8/14$

rate—a ratio that compares quantities of two different kinds
 A rate may be expressed as a percent (%), a decimal, or a ratio.
 Ex: The rate a swimmer swims $= \dfrac{\text{the distance covered}}{\text{time spent swimming}}$

ratio—the quotient of two numbers that is used to compare one quantity to another
 Ex: The distance (5 miles) someone runs in an hour (60 minutes) might be expressed as a ratio ($5/60$).

reciprocals—two numbers whose product is 1
 Ex: $1/3$ and $3/1$ are reciprocals.

reduced fraction—a fraction whose numerator and denominator are not divisible by any number other than 1
 Ex: $6/12$ can be reduced to $1/2$.

repeating decimal—a decimal in which the last digit or block of digits repeats without end
 Ex: $4.\bar{3}$ or 4.33333 . . .

terminating decimal—a decimal with a limited number of nonzero digits
 Ex: 4.32

Name

FRACTIONS & DECIMALS
SKILLS TEST

Each correct answer is worth 1 point. Total possible points = 100.

For 1-6, match the correct decimal letter (below right) with the written decimals (below left).

_____	1. forty-two thousandths	A. 4.42
_____	2. forty-two hundredths	B. 4.402
_____	3. forty-two ten thousandths	C. 0.042
_____	4. four and forty-two hundredths	D. 0.42
_____	5. four and four hundred two thousandths	E. 0.0042
_____	6. four and four hundredths	F. 4.04

7. Write the factors of 24. _____

8. Write the factors of 13. _____

9. Write the prime factors of 12. _____

10. Write the least common multiple of 4 and 5. _____

11. Write the least common denominator of $\frac{1}{7}$ and $\frac{4}{3}$. _____

12. Write the greatest common factor of 15 and 30. _____

13. Write all the common factors of 15 and 45. _____

14. Write all the common factors of 6, 18, and 24. _____

For 15-20, tell what place is in bold type by writing the correct letter.
(a) ones (b) tenths (c) hundredths (d) thousandths (e) ten thousandths

_____	15. 6.1372		_____	18. 31.004
_____	16. 4.011		_____	19. 9.09
_____	17. 0.266		_____	20. 16.207

For 21-26, write Y if a fraction is in lowest terms, or N if it is not.

_____	21. $\frac{7}{20}$		_____	24. $\frac{8}{15}$
_____	22. $\frac{11}{13}$		_____	25. $\frac{3}{39}$
_____	23. $\frac{9}{24}$		_____	26. $\frac{7}{21}$

Name _____

For 27-32, place these fractions in order from smallest to largest.

$\frac{1}{2}$ $\frac{2}{9}$ $\frac{1}{3}$ $\frac{3}{4}$ $\frac{2}{3}$ $\frac{1}{4}$

27. _____   30. _____

28. _____   31. _____

29. _____   32. _____

For 33-38, reduce each fraction to its lowest terms.

33. $\frac{12}{15}$ _____   36. $\frac{21}{49}$ _____

34. $\frac{16}{20}$ _____   37. $\frac{9}{45}$ _____

35. $\frac{9}{12}$ _____   38. $\frac{28}{42}$ _____

For 39-44, write T or F to tell whether each pair of fractions is equivalent.

_____ 39. $\frac{3}{5} = \frac{15}{25}$ _____ 42. $\frac{7}{12} = \frac{42}{60}$

_____ 40. $\frac{9}{12} = \frac{2}{3}$ _____ 43. $\frac{2}{3} = \frac{40}{66}$

_____ 41. $\frac{4}{22} = \frac{2}{11}$ _____ 44. $\frac{11}{15} = \frac{22}{33}$

For 45-49, round these decimals to the place in bold type.

45. 0.4632 _____

46. 173.06 _____

47. 0.275 _____

48. 12.0361 _____

49. 0.0055 _____

For 50-54, change the decimals to fractions or the fractions to decimals. (Round decimals to the nearest hundredth.)

50. $\frac{7}{12}$ _____

51. $\frac{2}{3}$ _____

52. 0.080 _____

53. 9.33 _____

54. 73.04 _____

For 55-59, change the fractions to percents. (Round percents to nearest whole percent.)

55. $\frac{3}{4}$ _____   58. $\frac{9}{5}$ _____

56. $\frac{7}{8}$ _____   59. $\frac{1}{5}$ _____

57. $\frac{9}{12}$ _____

For 60-71, change the decimals to percents and the percents to decimals. (Do not round any decimals.)

60. 0.36 _____

61. 14.7% _____

62. 1.950 _____

63. 0.56% _____

64. 27.261 _____

65. 3490% _____

66. 0.0795 _____

67. 7.36% _____

68. 0.0046 _____

69. 116.43% _____

70. 33.06 _____

71. 226.7% _____

For 72-81, solve the problems below. Write the answers on the lines. (Round decimals to the nearest hundredth.)

72. $1\frac{2}{3} + 2\frac{6}{10}$ _____

73. $\frac{9}{5} + \frac{2}{5}$ _____

74. 1.593 + 164.001 _____

75. $6\frac{3}{4} - 6\frac{3}{5}$ _____

76. $\frac{5}{13} \times \frac{4}{5}$ _____

77. $\frac{4}{5} \div \frac{7}{8}$ _____

78. 1.8 ÷ 0.36 _____

79. 22.7 x 66.66 _____

80. $2\frac{1}{2} \div 4\frac{2}{3}$ _____

81. $7\frac{1}{10} \times 1\frac{9}{5}$ _____

Name _____

For 82-92, write the answers on the lines.

_____ 82. Which of these fractions is smallest?
a. $\frac{1}{7}$
b. $\frac{2}{16}$
c. $\frac{2}{13}$
d. $\frac{3}{11}$
e. $\frac{4}{20}$

_____ 83. Which is the correct answer to this problem, in lowest terms?
$$\frac{3}{12} \div \frac{5}{9}$$
a. $\frac{27}{60}$
b. $\frac{15}{108}$
c. $\frac{9}{20}$
d. $\frac{5}{36}$

_____ 84. Which numeral below means sixty-six and sixty-six ten thousandths?
a. 66.066
b. 0.06666
c. 66.660
d. 66.0066

_____ 85. Which is the correct decimal for 19.076%?
a. 1.9076
b. 1907.6
c. 0.19076
d. 19.076
e. 190.76

_____ 86. Which fraction is in lowest terms?
a. $\frac{6}{21}$
b. $\frac{8}{4}$
c. $\frac{7}{49}$
d. $\frac{9}{11}$
e. $\frac{62}{4}$

_____ 87. What percent of 55 is 11?
a. 20%
b. 50%
c. 55%
d. 2%

_____ 88. What is the answer to 68.3 ÷ 0.01?
a. 0.683
b. 6830
c. 6.83
d. 683.0

_____ 89. What is the answer to 0.0422 x 0.001?
a. 422.001
b. 422,001
c. 0.00422
d. 0.0000422

_____ 90. 13 is what percent of 78? (Round to the nearest whole percent.)

_____ 91. What number is 75% of 120?

_____ 92. What number is 40% of 70?

For 93-100, solve these proportions to find x.

_____ 93. $\frac{3}{2} = \frac{x}{8}$

_____ 94. $\frac{10}{26} = \frac{x}{13}$

_____ 95. $\frac{15}{x} = \frac{5}{9}$

_____ 96. $\frac{12}{20} = \frac{36}{x}$

_____ 97. $\frac{x}{8} = \frac{20}{32}$

_____ 98. $\frac{10}{x} = \frac{30}{42}$

_____ 99. $\frac{21}{x} = \frac{7}{2}$

_____ 100. $\frac{27}{9} = \frac{42}{x}$

SCORE: Total Points _____ out of a possible 100 points

Name

FRACTIONS & DECIMALS
SKILLS TEST ANSWER KEY

1. C
2. D
3. E
4. A
5. B
6. F
7. 1, 2, 3, 4, 6, 8, 12, 24
8. 1, 13
9. 2, 3
10. 20
11. 21
12. 15
13. 1, 3, 5, 15
14. 1, 2, 3, 6
15. e
16. b
17. c
18. a
19. c
20. d
21. Y
22. Y
23. N
24. Y
25. N
26. N
27. $\frac{2}{9}$
28. $\frac{1}{4}$
29. $\frac{1}{3}$
30. $\frac{1}{2}$
31. $\frac{2}{3}$
32. $\frac{3}{4}$
33. $\frac{3}{5}$

34. $\frac{4}{5}$
35. $\frac{3}{4}$
36. $\frac{3}{7}$
37. $\frac{1}{5}$
38. $\frac{2}{3}$
39. T
40. F
41. T
42. F
43. F
44. F
45. 0.46
46. 173
47. 0.28
48. 12.0
49. 0.006
50. 0.58
51. 0.67
52. $\frac{8}{100}$
53. $9\frac{1}{3}$
54. $73\frac{4}{100}$ or $73\frac{1}{25}$
55. 75%
56. 88%
57. 75%
58. 180%
59. 20%
60. 36%
61. 0.147
62. 195%
63. 0.0056
64. 2726.1%
65. 34.90
66. 7.95%
67. 0.0736

68. 0.46%
69. 1.1643
70. 3306%
71. 2.267
72. $4\frac{4}{15}$
73. $2\frac{1}{5}$
74. 165.59
75. $\frac{3}{20}$
76. $\frac{4}{13}$
77. $\frac{32}{35}$
78. 5
79. 1513.18
80. $\frac{15}{28}$
81. $19\frac{22}{25}$
82. b
83. c
84. d
85. c
86. d
87. a
88. b
89. d
90. 17%
91. 90
92. 28
93. x = 12
94. x = 5
95. x = 27
96. x = 60
97. x = 5
98. x = 14
99. x = 6
100. x = 14

Basic Skills/Fractions & Decimals 6-8+

ANSWERS*

Some answers may vary slightly due to different rounding standards.

Page 10

1. $^4/_{14}$ or $^2/_7$
2. $^6/_{14}$ or $^3/_7$
3. $^5/_{14}$
4. $^3/_{14}$
5. $^{12}/_{14}$ or $^6/_7$
6. $^{14}/_{26}$ or $^7/_{13}$
7. Labradors $^{16}/_{68}$ or $^4/_{17}$
   Alaskan malamutes $^{25}/_{68}$
   hounds $^3/_{68}$
   Irish setters $^4/_{68}$ or $^1/_{17}$
   huskies $^9/_{68}$
   non-purebred mixes $^{11}/_{68}$

Page 11

1. $^{13}/_{20}$
2. $^1/_3$
3. $^{365}/_{500}$ or $^{73}/_{100}$
4. $^{295}/_{500}$ or $^{59}/_{100}$
5. $2^3/_4$
6. $^7/_{10}$
7. $^{98}/_{100}$ or $^{49}/_{50}$
8. $8^1/_2$, $9^1/_2$, $10^1/_2$
9. $^{723}/_{800}$
10. $^{10}/_{233}$
11. $^{108}/_{89}$
12. $^3/_1$

Page 12

1. Canada
   Jamaica
   Switzerland
   U.S.
   Russia
2. U.S.
   Russia
   Canada
   Jamaica
   Switzerland
3. U.S. $11^1/_2$ minutes
   Jamaica 11 minutes
   Switzerland $9^5/_6$ minutes
   Canada $8^5/_6$ minutes
   Russia $10^3/_4$ minutes
Canada is the winner.

Page 13

1. $2^1/_2$
2. $2^2/_3$
3. $3^1/_4$
4. $1^3/_8$
5. 3
6. $2^2/_5$
7. $3^3/_7$
8. $1^1/_2$
9. $7^1/_2$
10. $2^3/_5$
11. $^5/_4$
12. $^7/_4$
13. $^9/_4$
14. $^{11}/_5$
15. $^{14}/_5$
16. $^{21}/_5$
17. $^{11}/_{10}$
18. $^{15}/_{10}$
19. $^{31}/_{10}$
20. $^{23}/_8$

Page 14

1. 12 and 6 are composite; 2 is prime
2. 24 and 6 are composite; 2 is prime
3. 13 is prime
4. 36 is composite; 2 and 3 are prime
5. 21 is composite; 3 and 7 are prime
6. 28 is composite; 2 and 7 are prime
7. 56 and 8 are composite; 7 is prime
8. 63 is composite; 3 and 7 are prime
9. 48 and 12 are composite; 2 is prime

10-20.

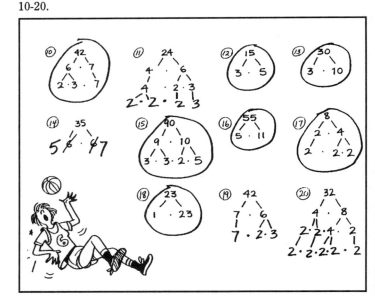

Page 15

1. G
2. O
3. O
4. S
5. E
6. __ blank
7. B
8. U
9. M
10. P
11. S
12. 3
13. 3
14. 4
15. 7
16. 8
17. 3
18. 9
19. 2
20. 5

Page 16

1. 8, 16, 24
2. 693
3. 18, 36
4. BJ King, S Lenglen, M Mallory, M Seles, J Fangio, T Watson, G Grafstom, W Bockl, D Jenkins, O Nepela, K Browning
5. 200
6. M Navratilova, S Graf, M Connolly, M Schumacher, J Nicklaus, B Hogan, G Player, K Schafer, G Grafstrom

Page 17

Famous saying is: "IT AIN'T OVER 'TIL IT'S OVER."
#s 7, 15, and 22 are apostrophes; #s 3, 9, 14, 19, and 24 are blanks.

Page 18

1. $^3/_5$
2. $^{15}/_{30}$
3. $^{45}/_{50}$
4. $^3/_{10}$
5. $^{19}/_{10}$
6. $^5/_{18}$
7. a. $^{15}/_{30}$
   b. $^{12}/_{52}$
8. $^{25}/_{110}$
9. $^{19}/_{11}$
10. $^{11}/_{44}$

Page 19

1. ½   20. 4/7
2. ¾   21. 5/6
3. 4/5   22. 2/3
4. ½   23. ¼
5. 1/3   24. 5/6
6. 1/3   25. 5/8
7. 1/3   26. ½
8. 4/5   27. 3/8
9. 6/7   28. 1/3
10. ½   29. ½
11. ¼   30. 2/9
12. ¾   31. no—½
13. ½   32. no—1/3
14. 1/6   33. yes
15. 2/5   34. no—1/7
16. 2/5   35. 1/3
17. 5/7   36. yes
18. 8/9   37. 2/3
19. 4/11   38. yes

Pages 20-21

1. 9¾ min.
2. 3 min.
3. 10½ min.
4. 82 yds.
5. 27½ yard line; closer to Franklin's goal
6. Larry 22 yds
   Kerry 14 yds.
   Joe 46 yds.
   Sam 31 yds.
7. yes
8. 48¼ yds.
9. 8 1/6 mins.
10. 8:30 P.M.
11. 9:10 P.M.
12. 53 2/3 yds.
13. 76 1/3 yds.
14. 10:00 P.M.

Page 22

1. individual 12 11/16
   personal 6 15/16
   group camping 8 15/16
   group cooking 5 1/16
   group food 4 11/16
2. Sally 6 3/8
   Mai 5 5/8
   Tamika 4 7/8
3. 16 7/8
4. 18 11/16
5. No; 1 13/16 lbs overweight

Page 23

1. 9000 ft
2. 1 (all of your body)
3. 30 mph; −41°
4. 15 mph
5. 300 ft
6. 55 degrees
7. 10 hours
8. 7½ minutes; 2 5/8 inches
9. 10 ft
10. 8¼ hrs

Page 24

1. mints 5 lbs
   pizza 20
   nuts 12 lbs
   punch 16 2/3 gallons
   cookies 10 lbs
   fudge 7½ lbs

2. hotdogs 4 4/5 lbs
   hotdog buns 4 dozen
   mustard 12 ounces
   ketchup 16 ounces
   hamburger 9 3/5 pounds
   hamburger buns 4 dozen
   potato chips 9 pounds
   baked beans 18 cups
   jello 2 pans
   ice cream 4½ lbs

3. hotdogs 16 lbs
   hotdog buns 13 1/3 dozen
   mustard 40 ounces
   ketchup 55 1/3 ounces
   hamburger 32 pounds
   hamburger buns 13 1/3 dozen
   potato chips 30 pounds
   baked beans 60 cups
   jello 6 2/3 pans
   ice cream 15 lbs

Page 25

Brianna's catch
  bass   112 9/128 ounces
  bluegill   49 7/8 ounces
  crappie   55 11/16 ounces

Simon's Catch
  bowfin   116 9/32 ounces
  catfish   356 89/128 ounces
  walleye   271 1/3 ounces

Nan's Catch
  bass   113 77/96 ounces
  bowfin   210 23/24 ounces
  crappie   49 23/64 ounces

Jason's catch
  bluegill   60 7/16 ounces
  catfish   389 3/8 ounces
  walleye   262 9/10 ounces

Page 26

Chili
  5¼ lb hamburger
  1 1/6 onion
  1¾ green peppers
  2 5/8 lb tomatoes
  3 3/8 T chili powder
  2¼ cans of beans

Potato Salad
  3 1/6 lb potatoes
  1 lb onions
  5/6 lb celery
  4 1/9 oz pickle relish
  4 eggs
  1/6 C mustard
  5/6 T salt
  7/12 T pepper
  ¼ T paprika

Apple Crisp
  6 lb apples
  2 5/6 lb brown sugar
  4 1/6 C oatmeal
  1 1/8 lb butter
  1¼ T cinnamon
  7/8 t. nutmeg

S'More Bars
  2 11/20 C crushed chocolate bars
  5½ C crushed graham crackers
  1/3 lb marshmallows
  3/8 C crushed peppermint candy

Page 27

Cars with these numbers will crash: 3, 4, 6, 7, 12, 16, 19, 20, 21, 23, 24, and 29.

Pages 28-29

0.12 — twelve hundredths
0.42 — forty-two hundredths
0.4 — four tenths
4.4 — four and four tenths
2.14 — two and fourteen hundredths
20.056 — twenty and fifty-six thousandths
33.583 — thirty-three and five hundred eighty-three thousandths
33.05 — thirty-three and five hundredths
4.87 — four and eighty-seven hundredths
0.44 — forty-four hundredths
0.08 — eight hundredths
0.8 — eight tenths
0.214 — two hundred fourteen thousandths
0.008 — eight thousandths
0.487 — four hundred eighty-seven thousandths
0.0487 — four hundred eighty-seven ten thousandths
3.305 — three and three hundred five thousandths
0.444 — four hundred forty-four thousandths
33.05 — thirty-three and five hundredths
3.35 — three and thirty-five hundredths

Page 30

July 1, 1980 — Oslo
Aug 31, 1979 — Crystal Palace
Aug 26, 1979 — Crystal Palace
Sept 20, 1978 — Oslo
June 26, 1977 — Crystal Palace
May 28, 1977 — Belfast
June 30, 1975 — Stockholm
July 17, 1974 — Haringey
July 25, 1973 — Motspur Park

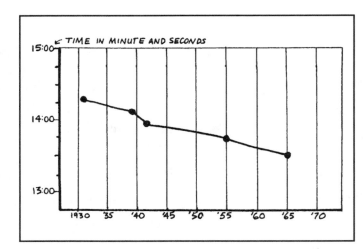

Page 31

1. a. millionths
   b. ten millionths
   c. hundred millionths
2. a. thousandths
   b. hundredths
3. a. hundredths
   b. tenths
   c. ones
4. a. tens
   b. ones
5. tenths
6. ones
7. hundredths
8. tenths
9. hundreds
10. ten millions

Page 32

1. 74.6 m
2. 10 sec.
3. 7.6 m
4. 8 m
5. 2.0
6. 7.4
7. 5.99
8. 9
9. 0.1
10. 41.1
11. 9.7
12. 400.1
13. 0.17
14. 2.65
15. 18.0
16. 4.99
17. 0.0
18. 45.9
19. 433
20. 87.12

Page 33

1. $587.54
2. $237.54
3. $462.98
4. $52.66
5. $120.05
6. $5.59; $4.41
7. $3.50; $1.50
8. $7.35; $12.65

Page 34

Melissa		
Dive	Sum of Scores	Final Score
back somersault	24.3	43.74
forward 1½ somersault	26	39
inward flying somersault	22.9	43.51
Total Score:		126.25

Tom		
Dive	Sum of Scores	Final Score
inward dive	23.6	40.12
forward double somersault	25.9	54.39
reverse somersault	22.9	45.8
Total Score		140.31

John		
Dive		Final Score
back double somersault		45.2
inward flying somersault		46.93
forward triple somersault		54.75
Total Score		146.88

Tina		
Dive		Final Score
reverse flying somersault		42.12
forward double somersault		44.31
inward double somersault		59.28
Total Score		145.71

Highest final score: John

Page 35

1. a. Time 0.44; Rate 29.09
   b. Time 0.43; Rate 29.77
2. a. Time 0.42; Distance 1.24; Rate 2.95
   b. Time 0.45; Distance 1.24; Rate 2.76
3. a. Time 1.11; Rate 12.07
   b. Time 1.00; Rate 13
4. a. Swim 0.16; cycle 4.24; run 2.65
   b. Swim 0.16; cycle 4.52; run 2.26

Page 36

1.

Player	DG	PSD
S. Valenko	0.240	0.333
T. Inqvest	0.375	0.429
J. Diskov	0.4	0.281
T. Beaufort	0.2	0.233
N. Tyler	0.166	0.192
M. Guilford	0.25	0.111

2.

Player	R/G	P/G	A/G
S. Valenko	1.7	3.3	1.1
T. Inqvest	1.55	3.33	1
J. Diskov	1.1	3.9	1.2
T. Beaufort	1	2.77	.88

N. Tyler   1.2   3.0   1.3
M. Guilford 1.4   2.88   1.11
3. Saves 14.9
    Goals 3.8

Page 37

QUOTE: "Float like a butterfly;
       Sting like a bee"

Page 38

1. a. 44.8%
  b. 7.8%
  c. 2.9%
  d. 0.9%
  e. 6.0%
  f. 5.5%
  g. 4.3%
  h. 6.5%
  i. 4.1%
  j. 1.6%
  k. 2.8%
  l. 12.8%

2. a. 0.061
  b. 0.155
  c. 0.143
  d. 0.780
  e. 0.098
  f. 0.093
  g. 0.197
  h. 0.038
  i. 0.282
  j. 0.487
  k. 0.255
  l. 0.534

Page 39

1. category	fraction/100	decimal	percent
a. 50s-60s	$8/100$	0.08	8%
b. 70s	$16/100$	0.16	16%
c. 80s	$28/100$	0.28	28%
d. 90s	$12/100$	0.12	12%
e. current	$36/100$	0.36	36%

2. category	fraction/100	decimal	percent
a. pop/rock	$28/100$	0.28	28%
b. country	$22/100$	0.22	22%
c. R&B/Rap	$18/100$	0.18	18%
d. Christian	$14/100$	0.14	14%
e. oldies	$12/100$	0.12	12%
f. classical	$6/100$	0.06	6%

Page 40

1. 38.4%
2. a. 25%
  b. 37.5%
3. a. 16.7%
  b. 55.6%
  c. 27.8%
4. 30%
5. 21.9%
6. a. 13.3%
  b. 53.3%

c. 33.3%
7. a. 37.1%
  b. 15.5%
  c. 20.6%
  d. 26.8%

Page 41

1. a. 50%
  b. 33⅓%
  c. 16⅔%
2. a. 19%
  b. 42.9%
  c. 38.1%
3. a. Tony 40.5%
  b. Jamie 28.6%
  c. Sheila 42.9%
  d. Jamie 71.4%

Page 42

1. 70
2. 23
3. 8
4. 17
5. 17
6. 61
7. 73
8. 12
9. 20
10. 56

Page 43

1. a. $7/12$
  b. $7/5$
2. $4/9$
3. $3/4$
4. $1/8$
5. a. $1/2$
  b. $5/2$
  c. $8/5$
  d. $1/2$

Page 44

1. a. 1055 meters per min
  b. 17.583 or $17\,7/12$ meters per second
2. 2 meters per second
3. 16 meters per second
4. a. 390 meters per minute
  b. 6.5 meters per second
5. a. 16.67 or $16\,2/3$ meters per second
  b. horse
6. 10.70 meters per second
7. 86 meters per second
8. 185.87 miles per hour
9. 461.54 feet per second

Page 45

1. $7/x = 1/50$; 350 m
2. a. $50/24 = 750/x$; 360 seconds
  b. $40/48 = 320/x$; 384 sec
  c. a, by 24 seconds
3. a. 32 seconds
  b. $5/x = 6/96$; 80 seconds

4. a. 322 seconds
  b. 320 seconds
  c. left, by 2 seconds
5. 7.5 cm
6. $16/48 = x/42$; 14th position

Pages 46-47

1. a. $x/1000 = 11/3$; x = 366.$\overline{6}$ ft.
  b. $x/3 = 2500/1000$; x = 7.5 cm
2. a. $x/2 = 350/15$; x = 46.67 lbs.
  b. $x/15 = 48/2$; x = 360 ft.
3. $x/1 = 200/75$;
  x = 2.6 carabiners (3 are necessary)
4. $x/1 = 85/15$; x = 5.67 camming devices
5. a. $x/75 = 9/2$; x = 337.5 ft.
  b. $x/2 = 1200/75$; x = 32 cm.
6. $x/14 = 1/4$; x = 3.5 light sticks (4 are necessary)
7. a. $x/1 = 500,000/1000$; x = 50 gallons
  b. $3/1,000,000 = x/1000$; x = 3000 ml
8. $x/1 = 160/50$; x = 30⅕ knots (31 knots)
9. $5/7 = x/420$; x = 300 minutes
10. $8/30 = 30.4/x$; x = 114 lbs.

Page 48

Correct answers with sky diver:
4, 5, 7, 8, 9, 12, 13, 14, 15, 16, 17, 22, 23

Incorrect answers with scuba diver:
1, 2, 3, 6, 10, 11, 18, 19, 20, 21, 24

Page 49

1. 4.87 sec
2. 24.17 sec
3. 1.64 sec
4. 126.30 sec or 2 min, 6.30 sec
5. 4.26 sec
6. 38.11 sec
7. 40.24 sec
8. 26.13 sec
9. 9.33 sec
10. 188.66 sec or 3 min, 8.66 sec

Page 50

1. 23%
2. 1.03
3. 10%
4. $40/187$
5. 2.2 seconds
6. 46
7. 14%
8. approx. 8800
9. 2 titles
10. 34,080,000 people